TWAYNE'S WORLD AUTHORS SERIES

A Survey of the World's Literature

Sylvia E. Bowman, Indiana University

GENERAL EDITOR

FRANCE

Maxwell A. Smith, Guerry Professor of French, Emeritus
The University of Chattanooga
Former Visiting Professor in Modern Languages
The Florida State University

EDITOR

Paul Eluard

TWAS 322

Paul Eluard

Paul Eluard

By ROBERT NUGENT

Lake Erie College

Twayne Publishers, Inc.   ::   New York

Library of Congress Cataloging in Publication Data

Nugent, Robert.
 Paul Eluard.

 (Twayne's world authors series)
 1. Eluard, Paul, 1895–1952—Criticism and interpretation.
PQ2609.L75Z78   841'.9'12   74-4132
ISBN 0-8057-2299-8

MANUFACTURED IN THE UNITED STATES OF AMERICA

Contents

About the Author

Robert Nugent received his A.B. from the University of California at Los Angeles, his B.L.S. from the University of California at Berkeley. In 1942 he studied Japanese at the Navy Language School at the University of Colorado and then served as a language officer with the First Marine Division in the South Pacific during World War II and in the occupation of Japan. After the war he studied and taught at Yale University where he received a Ph.D. in 1950, with a thesis on Baudelaire's literary reputation in France from 1867 to 1892.

Dr. Nugent was an American Field Service fellow at the University of Paris from 1948 to 1949. He has taught French at the University of California at Santa Barbara and, since 1956, at Lake Erie College, where he is now Professor of Modern Languages and College Librarian. He has also been visiting lecturer at Western Reserve University, giving seminars on Racine and Pascal.

He has published a translation of Sponde's *Sonnets on Love and Death*; a volume of poetry, *The Silent Voice*; numerous articles on French, Latin American, and Danish poetry in *The French Review*, *Hispania*, *Cithara*, *Renascence* and other literary reviews.

Preface

The poetic achievement of Paul Eluard is complex and diverse. Underlying this diversity runs a theme which unifies the various concerns of his verse into a coherent picture of the poet's universe. This theme is that of the poet's loneliness in particular, and of man's loneliness in general. My main purpose has been the discovery of how this solitude appears in the poetry. For this purpose, rather than attempting to understand Eluard's poetry through biography or through a pattern of development traced in terms of various periods, I have tried to block out the main threads of his verse, the warp and woof of his poetic fabric. In the end, hopefully, the reader will discover that loneliness which is, fundamentally, an encompassing view of reality.

Perhaps the most immediate reality for a poet lies in his relationship to his age; in Eluard's case this relationship found expression in the Surrealist revolution in literature and art. This revolution called for a review of a poet's role in society and—at the same time—for new responses in dealing with experience, in choice of subjects, in means of poetic expression. Chapter 1 will deal with Eluard and his age, in his attempt to find, within that revolution, a uniqueness of personal experience. Through a Surrealist aesthetic, he deepened two traditions of nineteenth-century poetry. Eluard continues the Romantic portrayal of the artist-poet, divorced from society by reason of his uniqueness and poetic sensibility; and that of the poet-seer who could give direction to society. For Eluard, these two portraits were intensified through his solitude, made more intense by way of a Surrealist search for originality. The second tradition, that of the artist-priest, from Baudelaire and the Symbolists on, gave rise—in Eluard's poetry—to a personal anguish, through a Surrealist experimentation which called for a total renewal of art.

To describe adequately and properly a seizure of reality, in these terms of poetic sensibility defined in relationship to his age, a poet must deal in images. A dilemma arises, which has its origins in Romanticism and which involves a poet's description of his own uniqueness. The achievement of the Romantic poets lay in their ability to invest the world with their own emotions— the distress of love, an awareness of some divine presence, the pain and torment of a feeling of loneliness, an awareness of self in its most intimate and revealing moments. Towards the middle of the nineteenth century, however, with Baudelaire, poets discovered that images found in nature had the power, in themselves, to signify emotions and ideas, with no attribution on the poet's part of such emotions and ideas. Eluard works within both points of view: The world appears to him poetic when it is perceived from his own isolation; the imagery of the world also appears to function apart from his own perception. "Images think for me" is an often quoted statement by Eluard. It implies both an awareness of the poet's individual poetization of the world and an absolute existence of imagery which does not depend on the individual poet. This problem will be dealt with in Chapter 2.

Once a poet, and especially a primarily visual poet such as Eluard, discovers how he sees the world and how he pictures the world, he must define for himself content and meaning. These have to do with basic emotions, help him to face solitude and to solve the problem of personal uniqueness. Eluard found that this varied spectrum of experience, especially that of love, could best be given a profound and moving expression through poetry. On the basis of these feelings, he could then proceed to form ideas or ideals of the world, and from this formalism work towards a theory of poetry and of the specific intent of words. These considerations will be discussed in Chapters 3, 4, and 5.

Eluard's world, moreover, is made up of not only an outside world together with an inner world of love for one individual, of ideas, of aesthetic preoccupations, but also of people. For Eluard the facts of experience were varied: Other than love, there was poverty, war, politics, the struggle for freedom; these latter were also the conditions of society. In Chapter 6, a discussion of his views on the human condition will show his

Preface

courage, his optimism, his convictions which made him one of the most popular of Resistance poets. All of these themes relate to tradition—the literary influences which acted upon his aesthetic.

Underlying the diversity of Eluard's poetic output can be found a theme which unifies this diversity into a coherent picture of the poet's universe. This theme is that of the poet's solitude in particular, and man's solitude in general. It has thus been my main purpose to discover how this loneliness appears in the poet's experience. For Eluard this vision is urgent and he succeeds in imparting to the reader the urgency of his vision.

ROBERT NUGENT

Painesville, Ohio

Acknowledgments

Grateful acknowledgment is made to Editions Gallimard for permission to quote from the work of Paul Eluard.

Chronology

1929 Meets Maria Benz ("Nusch").

1930 Surrealist crisis, after publication of Breton's *Second manifeste du surréalisme*. Eluard separates from Gala.

1932 *La Vie immédiate* (*Life Here and Now*).

1934 Marries Nusch.

1936 Participates in the International Exhibition of Surrealism (London, June 4-June 11); his lecture "L'Évidence poétique" published in *Surrealism* (ed. Herbert Read). *Les Yeux fertiles*.

1938 *Cours naturel*. Breton breaks with Eluard.

1939 Called to military duty. Returns to Paris, 1940.

1942 Reaffiliates with the Communist Party, because of anti-Fascist sympathies. Joins the underground.

1946 *Poésie ininterrompue. Le Dur Désir de durer* (*The Harsh Desire to Last*). Tragic death of Nusch.

1948 *Poèmes politiques*.

1949 Meets Dominique Lemor (who becomes his third wife in 1951) in Mexico where he attends the Congress of the World Council on Peace.

1952 *Les Sentiers et les routes de la poésie* (*The Paths and Roads of Poetry*).

1952 November 18: Paul Eluard dies of a stroke in his apartment near the Bois de Vincennes.

CHAPTER 1

Reality of the Self: the Poet and the Age

I Biography

PAUL Eluard was born December 14, 1895, in the northern
Paris industrial suburb of Saint-Denis.[1] He was thus the
oldest of the Surrealist generation (A. Breton, b. 1896, L. Aragon
and P. Soupault, both b. 1897, B. Peret, b. 1899). His family
background was that of *des gens simples*, the working class that
rises into the lower middle class. The family first moved to
Aulnay-sur-Bois, then to Paris in 1908. They lived in the rue
Louis-Blanc, the young Eluard went to school in the rue Clignan-
court. The poet always remembered this popular, working-class
background and environment. It inspired in him a tenderness,
a concern for human happiness, a quest for an answer to loneliness that inform his poetry. In this, Eluard's work bears a
resemblance to that of Camus, who also came from a similar
background and who also searched for a meaning to human
suffering.

In 1912, Eluard left Paris because of illness and spent two
years in a sanatorium in Davos, Switzerland. Here he met Gala,
who became the inspiration for his first love poetry. In 1914
he returned to Paris; with the outbreak of World War I he
entered the army. He continued to write poetry. In 1917 he
married Gala. This was the year also of two events which,
eventually, influenced Eluard's work: the beginning of the international Dada movement (*Dada* I, in Zurich, Picabia and the
revue *391*, in Barcelona, Reverdy and the revue *Nord-Sud*,
Paris); the taking over of power in Russia by the Bolsheviks.
He published poetry: *Le Devoir et l'inquiétude* (1917), *Poèmes
pour la paix* (1918) (which led to his friendship with the critic,
Jean Paulhan). In these two volumes are found themes that

15

dominate his poetry: love and the human condition. In 1918, his daughter Cécile was born.

After the war, Eluard, through his poetry, came into contact with the Paris literary scene of the early twenties: Paulhan, meeting with Breton, Aragon, Soupault. With these latter Eluard helped found the Surrealist movement. These were the years of Freudian influence (*Introduction à la psychanalyse,* 1918) and of interest in automatic writing (Breton discovered automatic writing in 1919). These two influences were reflected in Eluard's *Les Nécessités de la vie* (1920) and *Répétitions* (1922). A deeply experienced sense of division between tradition and experiment is apparent in *Mourir de ne pas mourir* (1924), a feeling of anguish and dismay with the world, which caused Eluard to abandon Paris and embark on a trip around the world. Shortly after his return to Paris appears *Capitale de la douleur* (1926), where the tone and imagery are primarily Surrealist, and Eluard becomes the recognized poet of Surrealism. In the same year appears *Les Dessous d'une vie ou La Pyramide humaine* (*The Reversals of Life, or The Human Pyramid*), in prose, where an element of fantasy and dreams is dominant.

Surrealism went through a crisis after the publication of Breton's *Second manifeste,* in 1930. At the same time Eluard went through a personal crisis, his separation from Gala, which led to his marriage with Nusch, in 1934. Eluard's poetry undergoes a change: From the Surrealism (dreams and fantasy), his poetry—inspired by Nusch—becomes one of participation in life, of the discovery of the real world, of two people. From *La Vie immédiate* (1932) through *Les Yeux fertiles* (*Fertile Eyes*), 1936, Eluard's interests concern humanitarian idealism, human happiness, especially in view of the Spanish Civil War (*Cours naturel* [Natural Flow], 1938. Eluard, as a sign of his reaffirmation of his feeling of solidarity with all men, had renewed his affiliation with the Communist Party; this lead to a break with Breton, who had just founded his *Fédération de l'art révolutionnaire indépendant* (1938).

After the outbreak of World War II, in 1939, and the armistice of June, 1941, Eluard entered the underground in 1942. During the Occupation Eluard became known as a poet of the Resistance, especially because of the poem "Liberté" (*Poésie et vérité* [*Poetry and Truth*], 1942. After the war Eluard became an international figure, traveling in Italy, Yugoslavia, Greece, Poland, leading to the publication of *Poésie ininterrompue* (*Uninterrupted Poetry*), 1946, a summing up of his search for happiness among men and for an answer to his solitude. In 1946, while in Switzerland, Eluard received news of the death of Nusch: The possibility of identifying love and life seemed no longer possible. During the years following, Eluard tried to deal with unhappiness, the problem of evil in the world, of how to come to a moral statement which would include a renewed faith in man and mankind (*Pouvoir tout dire*, 1951; *Le Phénix*, 1952). His meeting with Dominique (1949) and their marriage (1951) enabled Eluard to reaffirm his belief in human goodness, the possibility of love and an underlying moral structure in the world, especially evident in the posthumous publication *Poésie ininterrompue, II*. A heart attack in September, 1952, led to his death on the eighteenth of November.

II *Eluard and the Twentieth Century*

To understand a body of verse poses a question of what this poetry is or tries to be in relation to the age in which it is written. In general, and this has been true in the writing of verse since the Romantics, the production of poetry can be considered as either fulfilling a public function or a private one. Poetry can be thought of as a mirror of the age, a platform from which a poet comments on and clarifies various dilemmas—social, political, ethical—of his age. Or poetry can be, in effect, a purely private production, where the concerns are those of solitude, an experience of love, a search for a poetic understanding of the world. A poet thus becomes a guidepost of protest and of active participation in solving these dilemmas; or he chooses to clarify these concerns in his poetry.

Eluard, except in poems on the Resistance, made, I believe, the choice of a more private verse, a verse which reflects his own loneliness in the face of a world of cruelty and despair. His verse gains a stature it might not otherwise possess, because it does give the reader a feeling of a very moving personal experience. The poetry quite clearly shares in the milieu which gave it impetus; the milieu, however, does not dominate the poetic manner. Eluard, although one of the principal Surrealists in their striving for public acknowledgment and in the shock of much of their activity, remains a poet of personal, private anguish. Even when the themes he treats are of public concern —war, resistance to Fascist tyranny, the suffering of humanity— the poetry still has its origins in the poet's emotions over these concerns and in the solitude he experiences in facing them. Eluard's poetry does not arise from the demands of a group— political or other—that he express anger or indignation. In other words, with the possible exception of the last poems written after the reaffiliation with communism in 1942, Eluard's poetry has its primary and most characteristic point of departure in the private emotion.

Eluard's choice, however, did not prevent him from answering those larger questions of human suffering and world destruction, from which his personal anguish arose. His poetry, while re- maining private in tone, still offers the reader not only a criticism of life, but also an answer to the constantly vexing dilemma of man's mortality and freedom. In the poem entitled "Vivre" (*Le Livre ouvert*, I), for example, Eluard writes about life in general and his own life in particular, in terms of change and in terms of his loneliness, of how he defines and possibly overcomes this loneliness. Fundamentally, Eluard's poetry is an affirmation of life because of this change and the challenge to deal with solitude. The critic Gaston Bachelard has described Eluard's verse, stressing its organic, growing nature.[2] It is, first of all, a poetry which emphasizes the growing aspect of life, that life is a continual struggle to become more alive. In "Vivre," Eluard writes from the viewpoint of his solitude and of his need to find someone to share the solitude with him: *Nous avons tous deux nos mains à donner / Prenez ma main je vous conduirai loin* ("Both of us have our hands to give / Take my hand and I shall lead you far").[3] Implicit in this image is a structure of an ideal world, a humanitarianism, and a love, which illustrate a classic principle of organic life. To affirm life, the value of being alive, means that the struggle to survive, even when alone and when aware of the desire for communion with another person, has won out over a world which appears desolate. By means of poetry, the poet has come to dominate a world of distress and suffering. In "Vivre" Eluard continues:

> *J'ai vécu plusieurs fois mon visage a changé*
> *A chaque seuil à chaque main que j'ai franchis*
> *Le printemps familial renaissant.*

(I have lived several times my face has changed / On each threshold on each hand I have crossed / The family spring reborn.)

Here Eluard speaks to another person who, like the poet, stands alone, faced with the shifting circumstances brought about by time. He gives assurance that a rebirth from the prison, both of solitude and of time, is possible. Eluard speaks in his own voice and from his own experience, his innermost feelings and deepest emotions. For him, the commitment to his age must be described in terms of aloneness, of facing that aloneness. Eluard does not believe that it is necessarily absurd to try to break through to the other person. For him, this breakthrough is a part of a total system not only of change, but also of a paradoxical permanence of reestablishing and reaffirming values. In "Vivre," Eluard writes:

> *Gardant pour lui pour moi sa neige périssable*
> *La mort et la promise*
> *La future aux cinq doigts serrés et relâchés*
> *Mon âge m'accordait toujours*
> *De nouvelles raisons de vivre par autrui*
> *Et d'avoir en mon coeur le sang d'un autre coeur.*

(Keeping for him and for me the perishable snow / Death and the woman intended for me / The woman of the future with five fingers closed and open / My age always granted me / New reasons for living through others / And to know in my heart the blood of another heart.)

Eluard, then, views the human condition as one of constant change. He cannot speak either of himself or of others, except

in view of that change. It is, however, a significant part of
Eluard's optimism that he finds a constant renewal of faith, a
renewed vigor with which to face the day-to-day problems of
living in a changing world of human affairs. In the same poem
"Vivre," Eluard perceives a continuity in his own life (*Ah, le
garçon lucide que je fus et que je suis,* ["Ah, the lucid child I
was and am"]), a continuity based on how clearly he perceives
his own solitude and the necessity to overcome the being alone:
*Présence ma vertu dans chaque main visible / La seule mort
c'est solitude* ("Presence my strength in each hand I see / The
only death is solitude"). Thus Eluard's verse is optimistic in its
final estimate both of human values and of the human condition,
despite the threats which would extinguish the life of the individual as well as of the larger context—social, political, cultural—
in which the poet lives and which sustains him. More precisely,
the struggle with solitude leads to a positive and even useful
reassertion of life, one with a possibility of continued and
continual growth:

> De délice en furie de furie en clarté
> Je me construis entier à travers tous les êtres
> A travers tous les temps au sol et dans les nues
> Saisons passantes je suis jeune
> Et fort à force d'avoir vécu
> Je suis jeune et mon sang s'élève sur mes ruines. ("Vivre")

(From delight in rage from rage in lucidity / I build myself completely through all beings / Through all time on the ground and in
the clouds / Passing seasons I am young / And strong by dint of
having lived / I am young and my blood arises on my ruins.)

In these lines a reader finds the driving force of Eluard's
poetry, which is an awareness of life, a principle of experience
based on the deepest lines of self-exploration and self-fulfillment.
The expression of these directive forces—anguish, solitude, desire
for freedom, a reevaluation of the past—determine the nature
of his poetry. In a wider sense, moreover, this expression reflects
a spirit of the time in which he lives: The contemporary age of
anxiety, wherein the above-mentioned directive tendencies are

everpresent in a writer's mind, relates Eluard's poetry to his age.
In general, works of contemporary literature are answers to
this anguish and solitude. Camus, for example, whose work
mirrors a search for the "eternal summer" (*l'éternel été*), the
eternal life-giving force of sun, of plants, of sea, which would
rescue man from his captivity to an essence he had not earned,
a rescue brought about by an individual's defining his own existence through action. Proust, in *A la recherche du temps perdu*,
teaches us how we may understand and deal, through love,
friendship, music, painting, with the ever-recurring possibility
of loss of meaning in life when the death of some other person
occurs. Valéry's *Le Cimetière marin* makes the reader face
squarely his own death as well as that of others. For the existentialists any definition of the single individual is valid only after
that individual has confronted honestly and with no reservations
the fact of his peculiar mortality. And the theatre of the absurd
would give us an absolute condition wherein neither life nor
death possesses contingency and where we have time to act out
our inmost needs and desires. Eluard, in a like manner, tries to
act, tries to find meaning, is aware of death, and somehow
seeks out an absolute condition of truth and beauty. Eluard's
poetry treats these larger questions; his poetry, while remaining
poetic in tone, still offers the reader not only a criticism of life,
but also an answer to constantly vexing dilemmas of man's freedom. In searching for this answer, Eluard overcomes the loneliness which would tend to destroy him; the night of solitude
prepares the way for a day of community and oneness with
others: *la nuit qui prépare un jour interminable* ("a night which
prepares an interminable light of day" ["Vivre"]). His poetry
thus relates not so much to specific solutions to specific inci-
dents and concerns of the age, but more to a personal confronta-
tion with the anguish they bring about.

III   *The Significance of Revolt: Experiment and the Impulse toward Order*

With the cataclysmic upheaval of World War I, profound
social changes took place. Much has been written about this
war as marking a break between the nineteenth-century society

dominated and controlled by the cultivated middle class and the twentieth-century world of revolution and turmoil. The ensuing years have been ones of war, revolution, disaster, the atom bomb, and political dissensions; more specifically, for the artists during this period, revolt appeared to be inevitable. The generation which was to create the "new" art after the first World War could find no other identity than that of revolt and experiment. Against the backdrop of the destruction and bloodshed of the war, only revolt seemed stable, only experiment took on the familiarity of the usual. The initial literary impulse was nihilistic and apologetic of destruction—Dada.[4] Surrealism, in itself a revolt against the anarchy of Dadaism, tended to make the revolution into a firmer attitude of viewing and evaluating artistic creativity. Such revolt many times reached extremes which could not sustain a critical judgment or analysis of the poetry it gave rise to. Yet it made possible a powerful originality in the role of the image and opened the way to a far more significant stress upon the function of the artist and upon the artists as individuals.[5]

Eluard took part in the Surrealist revolution during the two periods of Surrealist activity: the first, during which Surrealism tried to find intellectual principles for the revolution (*la période raisonnante*, 1925–1930); the second, that period when the Surrealist movement achieved a kind of autonomy and liberty apart from the exigencies of the search for such reasons. In *Les Dessous d'une vie, ou La Pyramide humaine* (1926), Eluard attacked the existing order of things: It was order for the sake of order that made it impossible for the creative imagination to find expression. The feeling of malaise and social protest after the first World War did not make for any belief in a beneficial Providence. The world was definitely not God-directed nor God-centered. Man was reduced to his own solitude.

One way out from a feeling of individual isolation is through political action, a search for a basis of humanistic morality to which all men can subscribe. Around 1925, a division arose between Breton, who wished to continue the intellectual and aesthetic side of Surrealism, and those who wished to channel the spirit of revolt inherent in Surrealism towards the demands of a proletarian revolution. By 1933 Eluard had separated from affiliation with the Communist Party, protesting all the while against a middle-class morality based on property rights; he believed that such a morality imprisoned man and made true poetry impossible. In 1938, in a speech given at the London Surrealist Exhibition, Eluard stated: "True poetry is included in all that which has freed man from a ghastly sense of possession which has the face of death" (*La poésie véritable est incluse dans tout ce qui a franchi l'homme de ce bien épouvantable qui a le visage de la mort*).[6] For Eluard, the problem of writing verse was one of coming to terms with solitude, of reaching out towards others. Even those poems which are, seemingly, political in intent have as their origin Eluard's own feeling that individual loneliness could be overcome through affiliation with a political party.

Eluard's political convictions thus remained close to the humanitarian vision of an abstract utopia, where men would be close to others in common understanding of mutual needs. His concern is fundamentally moral; or, more precisely, Eluard is convinced that it is necessary for life to exist and to continue. His vision is essentially one of a total view of man's fear of being alone, of not being heard by others in moments of protest against tyranny and forces destructive of man's freedom. He believes that is the essential figure in the scheme of things. In "Le Droit le devoir de vivre" (*Poésie et vérité*), Eluard shows the reader a world without man; and that even when alone, it is that quality of being alone that enables man to hear and listen and be aware of the world about him:

> *Il n'y aurait rien*
> *Pas un insecte bourdonnant*
> *Pas une feuille frissonnant*
> *Pas un animal léchant ou hurlant.*

(There would be nothing / Not an insect buzzing / Not a leaf trembling / Not an animal licking itself or howling.)

Eluard then goes on to stress the nature of moral decision involved in man's solitary questioning of nature:

Rien de libre ni de gagner ni de fâcher
Ni de s'éparpiller ni de se réunir
Pour le bien ou pour le mal.

(Nothing free either to win or to spoil / Or to scatter or to gather together / For good or for evil.)

The poem concludes with an affirmation of the necessity of human life to give meaning to the world:

Il y aurait un homme
N'importe quel homme
Moi ou un autre
Sinon il n'y aurait rien

(There would be a man / No matter what man / Myself or another/ If not, there would be nothing.)

Furthermore, for Eluard, it is in order that human life be continued that civilization has significance. In "La Victoire de Guernica" (*Cours naturel*), his protest against the destruction caused by war equals Picasso's; like Picasso's painting, Eluard's poem makes clear how the havoc of war deprives man himself of his ability to understand the world about him: *Hommes pour qui ce trésor fut chanté / Hommes pour qui ce trésor fut gâché* ("Men for whom this treasure was sung / Men for whom this treasure was spoiled"). Misunderstanding, and more profoundly, revolt is a problem of conscience. In place of a world scheme of order and disorder, disorder comes to have a meaning of significance; disorder is understood in itself, and not because it is to be overcome in favor of a preconceived order of things. The individual, face to face with misunderstanding and alone as Eluard felt himself to be, undoubtedly experiences a need to define disorder, in terms similar to those later to be defined by the existentialists, as the absurd. The absurd (*l'absurde*) was the only order; hazard, chance, ruled the world. The absurd, moreover, could reconcile man to nature, which stood outside man himself, and to poetry, which came from inside man himself. Eluard could thus proceed from despair and anguish to hope and affirmation. As again in "Guernica," he can speak with confidence of the future:

> *Hommes réels pour qui le désespoir*
> *Alimente le feu dévorant l'espoir*
> *Ouvrons ensemble le dernier bourgeon de l'avenir.*

(Real men for whom despair / Feeds the fire that devours hope / Let us open up together the last bud of the future.)

As the existentialists do later, Eluard insists on the necessity of action and—in arising in one's anguish—of overcoming the frustration of private and solitary grief:

> *Pariahs de la mort la terre la hideur*
> *De nos ennemis ont la couleur*
> *Monotone de notre nuit*
> *Nous en aurons raison.*

(Pariahs of death the earth the ugliness / Of our enemies have the monotonous color of our night / We will triumph over them.)

The problem of individual conscience and action is also related to a notion of liberty. The notion of liberty gives meaning to all the tenets of Surrealism. ("The word liberty alone is all that yet exalts me," wrote Breton in the first Surrealist manifesto of 1924.) In the first place, freedom is defined as freedom from the overriding power of the conscious. Here the influence of Freud is to be taken into account. For Eluard, such liberation meant that the innermost striving of the subconscious to be free to express the deepest necessities of freedom and communication must be acknowledged. The subconscious recovered its rights and, especially, its aesthetic rights through the notions conceived or brought about in unconscious states. For Eluard this freedom signified not only liberty from an overpowering presence of nature and natural law and the liberation of instinct, but also a liberty to express those innermost feelings and emotions. These, then, could be a means of communication and eventual understanding with others, a means of freedom from a limiting solitude.

As is generally true of Surrealist doctrine, there is also the freedom given to the inner self, the *soi* (as distinguished from the *moi*). Here is the realm of the inner self, where love and death—according to Freud—seek to conquer each other. For Eluard, the struggle is more profoundly an assault on loneliness, on all that separates him from understanding the world and those who live in that world, rather than a struggle of private personal conflicts. And even poetry is a means of liberation, liberation from misunderstanding and the imprisonment of the self in its own solitude. Poetry becomes freed from the restraints of a previously imposed notion of an idea or an emotion. The image itself is, at long last, liberated and has come to take on the power of reason itself. Words, in themselves, propel reason; by the fact of speaking out to others, Eluard is more deeply aware of his solitary position, even the solitariness of his own intuition. This awareness is, in Bergson's words, the *élan vital* which brings about freedom.

The underlying belief in others becomes especially clear in the poems written during the Resistance. In the poem "Liberté" (*Poésie et vérité*) Eluard wrote:

> Sur mes cahiers d'écolier
> Sur mon pupitre et les arbres
> Sur le sable sur la neige
> J'écris ton nom.

(On my schoolboy notebooks / On my desk and the trees / On the sand and on the snow / I write your name.)

Eluard continues the list of objects: *Les cloches de couleurs, le fruit coupé en deux, la vitre de surprises* ("the steeples of color, the fruit cut in half, the window pane of surprises"). The technique, from one point of view, is a part of the general trend to separate the object from the intellectualized appreciation of the object. (Duchamp and Picabia had already, around 1912, begun *peintures-objets*, paintings which existed in themselves.) As in painting, rather than *composition after nature*, the principle of *autonomous structure* became the guiding principle of creative vision in poetry. Underneath the statement of artistic

manner, however, lies the notion of the destruction of the world
in order to rebuild a more complete and more real understanding of the world. And for Eluard this understanding had to
come from his own solitude; when he saw a world faced with
destruction, he could, from that destruction, re-think, re-see
the world and himself in it.

In the same poem "Liberté," Eluard also writes of natural
phenomena (*chaque bouffée d'aurore, le flot du feu béni* ("each
gust of dawn, the wave of blessed fire") on which he will
impose the name of liberty. Here Eluard appears to construct
a new spirituality, with an insistence on the creative instinct,
and outside the limits of a traditional apologetics. The freeing
of the deepest 'desire within the human being to create lies
at the root of Eluard's poetic temperament, because it is in the
very nature of this liberty to give man a way of coping with
his aloneness. Not only does this liberation require a clearing
away of the debris of the past, but also it creates from the chaos
a new, emergent world, a creation dependent on the artist alone
and not on divine prerogatives:

> *Et par le pouvoir d'un mot*
> *Je recommence ma vie*
> *Je suis né pour le connaître*
> *Pour le nommer*
> *Liberté*

(And by the power of a word / I begin again my life / I was born
to know it / To name it / Liberty.)

Eluard thus takes part in the tradition of the poet-seer, one
who sees a new world, who has visions of the hidden meaning
of reality. It is the peculiar achievement of Eluard's poetry that
he is able to combine all facets of experience in the visionary.
On one level, the visionary aspect is purely technical. The
object is seen to exist in itself: The secret of its hidden reality
is revealed in understanding the image in that part of the subconscious where the unique identity of the object is glimpsed.
The visionary outlook is also purely personal, in the sense that
it is in terms of a nonfunctional and refined state of awareness

that Eluard is able to deal with his solitude and to make others understand it and to come to it with understanding. Eluard affirms vision for vision's sake; and poetry was a means of living the vision itself. Eluard's conclusion is optimistic: a kind of eternal presentness of a profound and durable beauty in the world, that men were worth saving, and that eventually, in making the vision clear, there would be friendship and companionship between people. And in this final conclusion, he could come to terms with his own solitude.

CHAPTER 2

Reality of the World: the Poetic Image

I *The Terms of Vision*

THE primary question a poet must ask himself is how he is going to see reality and to define reality in terms of that vision. The real can be moral or religious, a conviction of a truth that informs his entire poetic outlook (as is the case of a religious poet like Claudel);[1] it can be a notion of things about him (tables, animals, roses) into whose life he must enter (as with Rilke). It can be the very profound awareness of his own life, of his own aloneness, as it touches that of others and of the external world. Eluard, in the title of a collection of poems published in 1921, *Les Nécessités de la vie et les consé-quences des rêves*, gives a clue to his concept of reality, or of how he conceives reality. He is preoccupied with living in the world, with being a part of its activities, meeting its demands; at the same time, his own personal inwardness, defined in terms of that aloneness, has to be recognized and given expression. These preoccupations were already evident in earlier volumes of verse published before 1921: *Le Devoir et l'inquiétude* (*Duty and Anguish*), 1917; *Poèmes pour la paix* (published separately in 1918); *Les Animaux et leurs hommes, les hommes et leurs animaux* (Animals and their Masters, Masters and their Animals), 1920. In the poetry of this period, Eluard's concern is with a contrast between the "living reality" of dreams and the "pure image" of the external world, between an inner purity of one's own solitude and a necessity of finding a corresponding purity in the outside world.

Since Baudelaire, especially, French poets had tried to find a pure image in the outside world; a poet then can refine from this discovery all dross of secondary considerations, either didactic or philosophic. The Romantics had first sought a pure reality,

29

distilled in an inner world of the psyche, in an effort to seize the image in itself, existing in itself and not dependent for its meaning on the relationships to external interests. Nerval, for example, had written of the secrets of the reality of the mind; Baudelaire had tried to seize the image as the key to the meaning of the refined existence, this purified reality. Rimbaud and Mallarmé continued and deepened the two streams of "refinement" and "purification." It is in Eluard's early poetry that he brings together these two tendencies.

In the early collection *Poèmes* (1914), in the poem beginning *Le Coeur sur l'arbre*, Eluard gives a series of moments of dream (*rêve*) where the inner vision makes clear the pureness of an image. In the first stanza, Eluard speaks of "the heart of the tree" where *le coeur* depends on the inner world. He associates this inner world, where he dreams of love, with the fulfillment of love. (The two themes become the principal subjects of his poetry around 1924.) The significance of the image *arbre* is that it indicates the focal point to which the inner concerns become attached: The act of thus narrowing the association between *coeur* and *arbre* (heart and tree) gives to the total image a stronger effect and therefore greater significance. The fusion of the two aspects of experience in a single phrase is *poesis*, the writing of the poem in itself. Eluard considers love in the light of the other person's action, *vous n'aviez qu'à le cueillir* ("You had only to pick it"). In other words, his solitude depends on another, experience is defined as two people alone who try to reach out to one another. Eluard also speaks of the pleasures and exaltations of love: *Sourire et rire, rire et douceur d'outre-sens* ("Smiling and laughing, laughter and sweetness beyond sense"). The duality and purity of love—*Vaincu, vainqueur et lumineux, pur comme un ange* ("Conquered, conquering and shining, pure as an angel")—gain meaning through identification of the experience of love with that quality of *arbre* which is most characteristic, its elevation: *Haut vers le ciel, avec les arbres* ("High towards the sky, with the trees"). The image *arbre*, moreover, takes on the purity of the experience of love.

In the second stanza of the same poem, Eluard again fuses the reality of his vision of the woman (. . . *une belle qui voudrait lutter / Et qui ne peut, couchée de la colline*, "a beautful woman

who would want to struggle / And who cannot, woman asleep
at the foot of the hill"), with the dual quality of the sky which
Eluard describes as *misérable* or *transparent*. The concept of
his love takes on the purified meaning of the sky; the sky, which
cannot struggle against itself and cannot become other than
it is, emphasizes the inevitable nature of the poet's love. In the
third stanza, Eluard speaks of "days" (*jours*): The furthest
extension of reality includes the added dimension of time; the
sense of time is existential, in that it is the experience itself that
time itself brings. Eluard equates the duality of experience,
taken in an almost moral sense of good and evil, with the
duality of the seasons (*Les fleurs sont desséchées, les graines
sont perdues, / La canicule attend les grandes gelées blanches,*
"The flowers are withered, the seeds are lost, / The heat of
summer is waiting for the great white frosts"). Again the psychic
reality of his experience becomes meaningful through the perception of the pureness of his vision of the world as it has a
beginning in his solitude.

In the fourth stanza, Eluard speaks of death, which, like
love or experience itself, has a dual nature. On the one hand,
Eluard emphasizes the blindness of death; to consider it otherwise is, in one way, to no avail and "decorative" (*peindre des
porcelaines,* "to paint china"). In another way, death has a
terrible beauty, like music, like *bras blancs tout nus* ("completely
bare arms") which can rise towards the sky or stretch out to
embrace the poet. An understanding of death underlies the
vision of the world where opposites (*les vents et les oiseaux,*
"the winds and the birds"), become one (*s'unissent*) and yet
where change is possible or even a necessary part of the world
(*le ciel change,* "the sky changes"). Yet in his working towards
a poetic image workable on all levels—present experiences,
their inherent dilemmas and solutions—Eluard is looking for
common denominators in experience which give a classic universality and timelessness to his images and which help him
to bear his aloneness.

Even in the most heartrending of experiences, war—with the
separation it brings about, the solitude, the memories of love—
peace, its opposite, becomes possible. The realization of peace,
in *Poèmes pour la paix*, is understood again, in terms of the

pure significance of images. The soldier-husband returning from war brings warmth as does the morning sun (*revient du soleil*); the images of war (*fusil, bidon,* "rifle, jerry can") are contrasted with the splendidness of the curving breast of the wife, the human face gains an importance through love and the happiness of love; the moon is associated with the beauty of the woman; a garden is like the poet's solitude, the poet works in this orchard and the source of life—the sun—burns also on the poet's hand, which in turn brings about the poem.

Again the consideration of reality is thus extended to include more than private association and private anguish. These emotions are in a constant state of tension because they can be dealt with only by means of an awareness of others. This awareness is seemingly impossible, because a poet writes from his aloneness. Reality, to be fully understood and adequately dealt with—even in a consideration of the nature of poetry—must include a preoccupation with fraternity; the enlargement of private concerns must expand towards a larger concept of fraternal love. In the collection *Pour vivre ici* (*In Order to Live on this Earth*), in the poem by the same title, Eluard again speaks from a viewpoint of solitude, of his aloneness (*l'azur m'ayant abandonné,* "the sky having abandoned me"). The poet makes a fire in order to have a kind of friendship and companionship; he shares with the fire the total experience of the day. Then he can say, *je vécus* ("I lived"); he experiences a feeling of containment, of oneness, of comfort within himself:

> *J'étais comme un bateau coulant dans l'eau fermée,*
> *Comme un mort je n'avais qu'un unique élément.*

(I was like a boat flowing in closed water, / Like a person dead I had only a single element.)

Further, the kind of reality in Eluard is a "seen" one, seen in the sense of capturing images and juxtaposing one against the other. He follows in this technique the Surrealist doctrine of free-association, not only for the primary purpose of aesthetics, but also for the purpose of getting hold of reality. From such control of the external real the poem grows, is itself creative, and reality takes on a depth—an extension into time—that relieves the poem from remaining on a single level of descriptive reality. Eluard is the most poetic of poets because his is a visual art or—more correctly—a visionary art. He perceives the *correspondances* between images. In "L'Amoureuse" (*Mourir de ne pas mourir*), for example, a "real" image is superimposed on a visionary one: *Elle est debout sur mes paupières* ("She is standing on my eyelids"). The image of the woman standing is a real image; the idea, however, that she might stand upon his eyelids, though real, is imagined. Throughout the poem the real image is thus amalgamated with the poet's proper self, the poetic self for whom the imagined is the real. In this fashion, the reality of the external world is made one with the reality of the poet's self, and the inner reality of his emotions becomes evident. Eluard, unlike Baudelaire, very rarely uses the adverb *comme* (like) and then only to reinforce the texture of an image:

> *Elle s'engloutit dans mon ombre*
> *Comme une pierre sur le ciel*

(She was engulfed in my shadow / Like a stone against the sky.)

The noun *pierre* gives a density to the verb, underscores the plunging notion of the verb; the noun *ciel* gives a dimension of depth and distance.

Eluard has defined a poem in the poem "Le Miroir d'un moment" (*Capitale de la douleur*). Poetry is a mirror, certainly. Yet Eluard's doctrine of the imagined real differs profoundly from the imitation of nature of neoclassical aesthetics. For the neoclassicists, following Horace, art was still a mirror, still an imitation, a refabricating as closely knit as possible on the original model. For Eluard, the use of the mirror is far more intimate; the reader sees into the mirror, the mirror is the image itself which holds, as does the mirror, truth. (The problem of appearance and reality will be discussed later in the chapter on the reality of the mind and of the idea.) The essence of Surrealist doctrine is the truth of the mirror itself; a kind of reversal is operative: not the holding up of the mirror to nature by the poet, but the image in itself constitutes a mirror. In "Le

Miroir d'un moment,"[2] the mirror has several functions: It breaks up light, the light that might distort (*il dissipe le jour,* "it dissipates the light"); it shows the unconnected images of appearances, those images which are implicitly joined but appear to be unjoined (*il montre aux hommes les images déliées de l'apparence,* "it shows men images which are freed from appearance"). The image is deprived of softness: *dur comme la pierre, / La pierre informe, / La pierre du mouvement et de la vue* ("hard as stone, shapeless stone, The stone of movement and of sight"). The image shows up truth, takes away hypocrisy; it has thus a very definite moral function, a kind of moral pragmatism which underlies Eluard's constant anguish over the nature of man's relationship with others, which relationship should be one of truth and forthrightness, even though everyone stands alone. This pragmatism, moreover, helps to overcome feelings of anguish and solitude.

Eluard's intent, however, is never moralistic; the value of the experience of an image resides in the image itself: *Ce que la main a pris dédaigne même de prendre la forme de la main* ("That which the hand took even disdains to take on the form of the hand"). The image exists purely, with no intellectualization, only the living reality of the image itself:

> *Ce qui a été compris n'existe plus,*
> *L'oiseau s'est confondu avec le vent,*
> *Le ciel avec sa vérité,*
> *L'homme avec sa réalité.*

(That which had been understood no longer exists, / The bird has become one with the wind, / The sky and its truth, / Man and his reality.)

Eluard thus reaches a definition of his solitude through a definition of the image. Solitude is simply the reality which is man himself, just as any part of nature is defined by its self. The real self, for Eluard, is his being alone.

II   *The Reality of the Imagination*

The reader then wonders, in reading and studying the poems, what part does reality of the imagination play in a poet's life.

In "Nuits partagées" (*La Vie immédiate*) he writes: *Je m'obstine à mêler des fictions aux redoutables réalités* ("I insist on mixing fictions with fearful realities"). He populates *maisons inhabitées* ("empty houses") with *femmes exceptionnelles* ("exceptional women"). He defends such imaginative fiction by a reason which is similar to Valéry's *charme*. In order to sing of objects, in order for them to be poetic, Eluard must discover them again in a kind of poetic invention: *Objets inutiles, même la sottise qui procéda à votre fabrication me fut une source d'enchantement* ("useless objects, even the stupidity which preceeded the making of you, was a source of enchantment for me"). He conquers the indifferences of *êtres indifférents* and seems to force a recognition of his solitude. Like Baudelaire, Eluard discovers in a world of poetic fancy a habit of poetry: *J'ai pris l'habitude des images les plus inhabituelles. Je les ai vues où elles n'étaient pas* ("I got into the habit of the most unaccustomed images. I saw them where they were not"). All that surrounds us is reinvented through such magic—streets, squares, women. In a way, such reinvention is a protest against reason: *La raison, la tête haute, son carcan d'indifférence, lanterne à tête de fourmi, la raison pauvre mât de fortune pour un homme affolé, le mât de fortune du bateau* ("Reason, with its head high, with its iron collar of indifference, ant-headed lantern, reason poor mast of fortune for a maddened man, mast of fortune of the boat"). Reason often misdirects awareness towards another end than understanding. Reason cannot give understanding, although it can help explain to others what is understood intuitively.

Poetic fancy, moreover, depends on the compulsiveness of any word or words which come to mind. The role of reason, in the perception of reality, is to seize upon the verbal situation which imposes itself upon the poet. The reader might compare Eluard's practice with Valéry's. Valéry writes of inspiration as follows:

The poet is awakened in man by an unforeseen event, an incident outside or within himself: a tree, a face, a "topic," an emotion, a word. At times, it is a desire for expression (*volonté d'expression*) which begins the game, a need to translate that which is felt; at other times, it is, on the contrary, an element of form, a sketch of an ex-

pression (*esquisse d'une expression*) which seeks its cause, which
seeks a direction in the space of my soul. . . . Observe this possible
duality beginning the action: sometimes some means of expression
wants something that it can serve.[3]

In Eluard's poetics, however, this distinction is not made. The
volonté d'expression is identical with the *esquisse d'une expression*. Both arise from the same kind of thinking about, or
reasoning with, the image in itself; the image wills the ex-
presssion and the expression, which is itself the image, wills the
image. Much more is involved than inspiration, much more than
Ronsard's possession by poetic madness (*je suis troublé de fureur,*
"Ode à la Reine," 1550), much more than the melancholy Mus-
set experiences in writing verse (. . . *quelle singulière et triste
impression / Produit un manuscrit,* "Dédicace" to *La Coupe et
les lèvres*), much more even than Valéry's inescapable fatalism
of purity:

> *Je touchais à la nuit pure,*
> *Je ne savais plus mourir,*
> *Car un fleuve sans coupure*
> *Me semblait me parcourir . . .*
>   ("Poésie," *Charmes*)[4]

(I touched upon the fine night, / I was no longer able to die, /
Because a seamless river seemed to run through me.)

For Eluard there exists both an aspect of intellectual discovery—poetic rationalization—and the surprise of the action
itself. The poem "L'Univers solitude" (*A toute épreuve* [*Holding Fast*]), though concerning the experience of love, uses a
comparable notion of the experience of poetry as a means of
expression; the two experiences are eventually welded together.
Eluard writes:

> *Le corps et les honneurs profanes*
> *Incroyable conspiration*
> *Des angles doux comme des ailes*
> *—Mais la main qui me caresse*
> *C'est mon rire qui l'ouvre*

> *C'est ma gorge qui la retient*
> *Qui la surprise*
> *Incroyable conspiration*
> *Des découvertes et des surprises.*

(The body and profane honors / Unbelievable conspiracy / Of angles sweet as wing. / —But the hand which caresses me / It is my laughter which opens it / It is my throat which holds it / Which quells it / Unbelievable conspiracy / Of discoveries and surprises.)

The element of poetic inspiration is similarly dual: both *découvertes* (acts of the reason of the will) and *surprises* (the given moment of pleasure forced upon one when the will is in abeyance).

The underlying theory of the identification of the two roles of images is given in "Identités" (*Cours naturel*).[5] For Eluard all life has a unity which constitutes the basic unity of his work. All aspects of reality, the subjects of images, are seen in the same light:

> *Je vois les champs la mer couverte d'un jour égale*
> *Il n'y a pas de différence*
> *Entre le sable au bord qui sommeille*
> *La hache au bord de la blessure*
> *Le corps en gerbe déployé*
> *Et le volcan de la santé.*

(I see the expanse of the sea covered by an even light / There is no difference / Between the sand which sleeps / The axe on the edge of the wound / The body unfolded as a sheaf of corn / And the volcano of well-being.)

Basically Eluard's approach is moral:

> *Les fêtes sans reflets les douleurs sans écho*
> *Des fronts des yeux en proie aux ombres*
> *Des rires comme des carrefours*
> *Les champs la mer l'ennui tours silencieuses tours sans fin.*

(Holidays without gleams of light sufferings without echo / Foreheads eyes which are prey to shadows / Sound of laughter like city squares / The fields the sea boredom silent towers endless towers.)

The enlargement of a purely aesthetic notion becomes a moral preoccupation. This enlargement reflects a distress over personal solitude, the ultimate world where the poet must operate. Eluard continues (in "Identités") a tradition of the nineteenth century, that of romantic solitude:

> Je vois je lis j'oublie
> Le livre ouvert de volets fermés.

(I see I read I forget / The open book of my closed shutters.)

In "Blason des fleurs et des fruits" (*Le Livre ouvert* [*The Open Book*], II) Eluard takes up an older poetic form, the *blason*, and uses it for his own purposes. The poem begins with the statement:

> A mi-chemin de fruit tendre
> Que l'aube entoure de chair jeune
> Abandonnée
> De lumière indéfinie
> La fleur ouvre ses portes d'or.

(Half-way on the tender fruit / That the dawn surrounds with young flesh / Abandoned / By the undefined light / The flower opens its golden gates.)

The poem is structured musically, with refrains that amplify the connection with his own solitude; the idea of the death of love (*Poème plein de frondaison / Perle morte au temps du désir*, "Poem full of foliage / Pearl dead at the time of desire"); the passing of pleasure (*Marguérite l'écho faiblit / Un sourire accueillant s'effeuille*, "Daisy the echo weakens / A welcoming smile sheds its petals"); the oneness, akin to worship, of the life force that informs all characteristics of nature that are available for poetry (*Dans le filet des violettes / La fraise adore le soleil*, "in the net of violets / The strawberry worships the sun"); the harshness of life, which is the necessary counterpoint to the adoration of life (*Mure fuyant entre les ronces / Aster tout saupoudré de guêpes*, "The blackberry fleeing among the brambles / The aster all powdery with wasps"). In all of these *blasons,* however, the poet is forever tied, bound, to his own solitude:

> *J'ai beau vous unir vous mêler*
> *Aux choses que je sais par coeur*
> *Je vous perds le temps est passé*
> *De penser en dehors des murs.*

(To no avail I bind you / To the things I know by heart / I am losing you the time is past / To think beyond the walls.)

The impossibility of external attributes corresponding to an absolute reality of the images parallels the impossibility of the poet's attributing to these images his own escape from solitude.

The problem lies in understanding reality and in appreciating reality; it is essentially one of communication. In "La Halte des heures" (*Le Livre ouvert,* II), Eluard writes:[6] *Immenses mots dits doucement* ("Immense words spoken quietly"), and describes the quiet power of these words:

> *Grand soleil les volets fermés*
> *Un grand navire au fil de l'eau*
> *Ses voiles partageant le vent.*

(Bright sun closed shutters / A big ship going with the current / Its sails sharing the wind.)

They have the qualities of dream; their capacity is to bring opposites together:

> *Et les saisons à l'unisson*
> *Colorant de neige et de feu—*
> *Une foule enfin réunie.*

(And the seasons in unison / Staining with snow and fire— / A crowd brought together at last.)

For it is within the structure of imagery that the poet lives. The structure is, moreover, not only an internal one of private feeling, but also one of a visual experience. It therefore has, at the same time, a reality with two possibilities of poetic expression, the visual and the emotional. In "Le Cinquième poème visible" (*A l'Intérieur de la vie* [Within Life's Limits]), Eluard writes: *Je vis dans les images nombreuses des saisons / Et des années* ("I live in the numerous images of the seasons / And the years"). Within time the poet weaves the fabric of his poem from the variety of images time produces. He sees all around him sources of poetic imagery: *Je vis dans les images innombrables de la vie / Dans la dentelle / Des formes des couleurs des gestes et des paroles* ("I live in the innumerable images of life / In the lace / Of forms, colors, gestures, words"). Again the intention is moral: *Je vis dans la misère et la tristesse et je résiste / Je vis malgré la mort* ("I live in misery and sadness and I hold out / I live in spite of death").

The poem constitutes a series of images, each corresponding to an emotional quality. Eluard does not attempt to equate his emotional state with the image; he refuses to give way to the pathetic fallacy. Rather he uses images, words, which stand as kinds of symbols for qualities. He is surrounded by people who are looking for, seeking out, answers. He employs the image of a river:

> *Je vis dans la rivière atténuée et flamboyante*
> *Sombre et limpide*
> *Rivière d'yeux et de paupières.*

(I live in the river which is diminished and blazing / Dark and limpid / River of eyes and eyelids.)

To indicate the dual quality of his existence, Eluard uses contrasting images:

> *Je vis en même temps dans la famine et l'abondance*
> *Dans le déarroi du jour et dans l'ombre des ténèbres.*

(I live at the same time in famine and abundance / In the disarray of light and in the order of shadows.)

Though summoned by images, which speak to him (as do images in Baudelaire's "Les Correspondances") Eluard still accepts what we may call day-to-day life:

Malgré la mort malgré la terre moins réelle
Que les images innombrables de la mort
Je suis sur terre et tout est sur terre avec moi
Les étoiles sont dans mes yeux j'enfante les mystères
A la mesure de la terre suffisante.

(In spite of death in spite of the earth less real / Than innumerable images of death / I am on earth and all is on earth with me / The stars are in my eyes and I give birth to mysteries / In tempo with the adequate earth.)

Within the real structure of images in Eluard there is a kind of *élan vital*, a giving of life to the image as the image gives life to the poet. He does not achieve this by comparison. He does so, rather, in the fashion of Baudelaire, by seizing upon one aspect of nature (a person, a thing, an animal even) which has the inherent qualities that the poetic emotion of the poetic situation demands. This structure, moreover, is physical. In "Tout dire" (*Tout dire* [*To Tell Everything*]), to express the quality of freedom, Eluard uses the most homely and the most physical of objects:

Pourrai-je dire enfin la porte s'est ouverte
De la cave où les fûts mettaient leur masse sombre
Sur la vigne où le vin captive le soleil
En employant les mots du vigneron lui-même.

(Will I be able, then, finally, to say that the door has opened / From the cellar where the casks placed their somber mass / On the vine where the wine makes captive the sun / By using the words of the wine-grower himself.)

The idea of the cellar, the casks, the labor of the vineyard and the growth of the vines, all suggest the acquiring of growth, of something solid being achieved. It is not a question, I believe, of Eliot's objective correlative, which would make of the poem a duality, saying one thing on the verbal level, and implying another on the moral. There is far more feeling and emotive implication in Eluard, the objects correlated constitute not only the poetic situation but also make up a part of the poet's life itself. In other words, Eluard's poetry is far less intellectualized, far more natural, and, in this sense, direct, than, for example, is the poetry of Eliot. There is far more, in Eluard, of movement, of life, of actual *présence* of the image. In the passage just quoted, the image of the door opened is much more an *image vécue*; the notion of captivity (with so many memories of the past), is here construed in the sense of the vine capturing the sun, so that a sense of physical presence is experienced. It is this capacity of association, of tying together—in a living and organic whole—that gives strength to Eluard's poetry. In "Printemps" (*Le Phénix*) [*The Phoenix*],[7] the reader perceives a deepening of the emotional significance of a commonplace poetic notion, the idea of the rebirth of spring. Eluard begins with an enumeration of the qualities of spring:

> *Il y a sur la plage quelques flaques d'eau*
> *Il y a dans les bois des arbres d'oiseaux*
> *La neige fond dans la montagne*
> *Les branches des pommiers brillent de tant de fleurs*
> *Que le pâle soleil recule.*

(There are on the beach several pools of water / There are in the woods trees sweet with birds / The snow is melting on the mountain / The branches of the apple trees sparkle from too many flowers / That the pale sun drags back.)

III   *The Living Function of Imagery*

The significance of images, for Eluard, lies in his ability to create reality visually and to attribute such a recreated and reappreciated reality to the woman he loves (*je vis ce printemps près de toi l'innocente*, "I live this spring near to you, woman of innocence"); Eluard enlarges the visual capture of spring to include a statement of value (*Rien de ce qui périt n'a de prises sur toi*, "Nothing which perishes has hold over you"). The capability to revive the image, in the etymological sense of reliving the image, is the basis of Eluard's poetic choice of image. He has entitled a volume of poetry, *La Vie immédiate*, and it is this urgency of an immediacy of perception that allows an image to function organically in a poem. In the prose poem "Nuits partagées" (from *La Vie immédiate*), Eluard writes:

> *Quand j'arrive, toutes les barques s'en vont, l'orage*
> *recule devant elles. Une ondée délivre les fleurs*
> *obscures, leur éclat recommence et frappe de nouveau*
> *les murs de laine.*

(Whenever I arrive, all the boats leave, the storm draws back before them. A wave delivers the dark flowers, their brilliance begins again and strikes anew the walls of wool.)

The verbs are in the present tense, giving both an immediacy and an eternity to the actions. The maritime image, as in Baudelaire, gives an impression of vastness, of *voyage*. There is also a feeling of calmness and tenderness. Parallel with the maritime image is that of a shower which causes the flowers to shine against "the fuzzy garden walls." Both are organic images, dealing with natural phenomena. Both, moreover, are essential to the feeling tone the poet wishes to establish. They are, additionally, delivered from a kind of monotony of tone, of flatness of expression, not only by their liaison with the feeling, but more especially through a kind of "aesthetic distance" or *élévation* that is found in Baudelaire. The poet looks at these images, the poet's eye inspects them, as from above, almost omnisciently. The peculiar combination of intimacy of feeling and aloofness reminds the reader of Baudelaire.

The poem in Eluard's work is relieved from a static quality of mere description by the verbs, which are—for the most part—verbs of action. In "Nous sommes (*Chanson complète* [*Total* Song]), Eluard gives the image visually, calls upon the reader to participate in the movement of the image: *Tu vois le feu du soir qui sort de sa coquille / Et tu vois la forêt enfouie dans ta fraîcheur* ("You see the fire of evening which comes out from its shell / And you see the forest hidden in your freshness"). The contrast between the verb *sort* and the past participle *enfouie* gives an impression of action, both past and present. This invitation to the reader to participate visually and actively in the poem expands the reader's vision; not only is it

a momentum or surface participation, but one in depth, one
which calls upon the reader to restate to himself the use of
images and their significance and to reevaluate for himself a
kind of moral grandeur:

> *Tu vois la plaine nue aux flancs du ciel traînard*
> *La neige haute comme la mer*
> *Et la mer dans l'azur.*

(You see the bare plain with the sides of the laggard sky / The
snow high as the sea / And the sea high in the blue heavens.)

It is a kind of discovery, a kind of transformation of reality.
Frequently the reality of the image is based on physical, bodily,
characteristics. It is a poetry of physical concreteness: *Des
hommes de dessous les sueurs les corps les larmes / Mais qui
vont cueillir tous leurs songes* ("Men are underneath sweat
bodies tears / But who are going to gather all their dreams").

As in Baudelaire, the preoccupation with the physical is
associated with the spiritual. Eluard is obviously not a Catholic
poet the way Baudelaire is. Nor does Eluard tend towards
Manichaeism, especially in his view of love, as does Baudelaire. Eluard accepts both the spiritual and the physical sensitivity; the two feelings are linked by chains of concerns for
the woman he loves, for mankind. Together, they lead towards
an understanding of suffering, loneliness, spiritual anguish, and
desolation. Eluard, as does Baudelaire, discovers in the physical
presence of the person loved a true beauty, profound and
moving, one that he would not willingly discard in favor of another; the reader asks himself if this beauty is a step, as on the
Platonic ladder, towards a supernatural beauty. The function of
the image is to imply such a function:

> *Au son d'un chant prémédité*
> *Tout son corps passe en reflets en éclats*
> *Son corps pavé de pluie armé de parfums tendres*
> *Démêlé le fuseau matinal de sa vie.* ("Médieuses," *Médieuses*)

(At the sound of a premeditated song / All her body passes in
reflections in outbursts / Her body paved with rain armed with
tender perfumes / Unwound the matinal distaff of her life.)

The appeal to all the senses is in the *lignée* of Baudelaire and Valéry. There is the auditive (*chant*); visual (*reflets, éclats*); olfactory (*parfums tendres*); touch (the image of the unwinding distaff, an action performed by hands); even, in a way, taste (the moisture implied in *pluie* associated with *corps*). Eluard's imagery, as does Baudelaire's, works on all these levels. The total impression is one, in Baudelaire's phrase, of *luxe, calme* et *volupté*.

IV   The Universe of Images

In a total envisioning of reality, a problem arises: Where does a poet fit into this scheme of universal beauty based on the immediate sensations? Eluard places himself in the middle of the universe he has thus created; he tries to identify himself by placing himself visually in the center of the image. In the poem "Médieuses," Eluard writes:

> *Près de l'aigrette du grand pont*
> *L'orgueil au large*
> *J'attends tout ce que j'ai connu*
> *Comblée d'espace scintillant*
> *Ma mémoire est immense.*

(Near the crest of the big bridge / Pride spread wide / I await all that I have known / Filled with shining space / My memory is immense.)

Eluard speaks here through the figure of the *médieuse*, or a myth of woman; in a Valéryean sense, as does Valéry in *La Jeune Parque*, Eluard describes himself. In the midst of his own solitude, in a complete *dénuement* of all other accompanying emotions, the poet waits. He is "filled with shining space," he has become one with the world which is the real source of his poetic imagery. It is the *je universel* that Pierre Emmanuel finds in Eluard.[8] The poet's memory thus becomes the memory of the universe, and this memory, in turn, informs the imagery of the world. The imagery in the poems contains a perception of universality. Although Eluard does not attempt to teach, he does wish to know some kind of reason why the world was

created. Eluard does not think as does Valéry. Eluard's images
always try to prove an affirmation of the principle of such
knowledge. His poetry many times can be read and understood
as the story of how a poet seeks knowledge. Underneath the
surface of the images, the reader comes upon a biographical
element of Eluard's search in this respect, which is related to
mémoire, but is closer to *souvenir.* In "Vivre" (*Le Livre ouvert,*
I), Eluard writes:

> *Ah le garçon lucide que je fus et que je suis*
> *Devant la blancheur des faibles filles aveugles*
> *Plus belles que la lune blonde fine usée*
> *Par le reflet des chemins de la vie.*

(Ah the clear-minded boy I was and am / In front of the whiteness
of the weak blind girls / More beautiful than the blond delicate moon
worn out / By the reflection of the roads of life.)

The implicit humanity of the image is typical of Eluard,
his participation in the human condition that is a constant theme
of his verse. The creation of an image, according to Surrealist
belief, is a product of the mind, a completely private image,
pure in its spontaneity, oneiric in its origin. True Surrealist
doctrine would deny, as had André Breton, that poetry—as
imagery founded on the reality of the world—served a function
beyond its own adventure. In the poem just quoted, Eluard,
I think, goes beyond true Surrealism and shows a deep desire
to help men by his example and his courage. It is true that many
poems by Eluard exist only as a kind of spontaneous illustrations
of what the poet is feeling at the moment, the more or less
confirmed "picture" in the mind. Much Surrealist art is in this
vein; Picasso and Dali illustrated books for the Surrealist writers.
Yet I am convinced there is a deeper belief in Eluard. While
maintaining the mystery of the image, Eluard refuses to create
literature (especially in the sense of Romantic, poetic pose)
and wishes always to be a part of others' lives. In "Vivre"
Eluard writes:

> *Présence ma vertu dans chaque main visible*
> *La seule mort c'est solitude*

Du délice en furie de furie en clarté
Je me construis entier à travers tous les êtres
A travers tous les temps au sol et dans les nues
Saisons passantes je suis jeune
Et fort à force d'avoir vécu
Je suis jeune et mon sang s'élève sur mes ruines.

(Presence my virtue in each visible hand / The only death is solitude / From delight to madness from madness to light / I build
myself anew complete through all beings / Through all times on the
ground and in the clouds / Passing seasons I am young / And strong
by dint of having lived / I am young and my blood rises as from
my ruins.)

Thus Eluard's poetry does not end up in nihilism as was true
of the Dadaist experiments. His effort is not to destroy, but to
build up. It is true that he reduces the appearance of things,
objects, nature, even people in a kind of process of volatiliza-
tion. The earlier experiment called pure poetry was a purification in that it was similar to a chemical reduction to the purest
essence of the thing, as in Mallarmé, or to the purest intellectual
perception, as in Valéry. In Eluard, however, *le mot pulvérisé*
("the pulverized word") is reconstructed: *je me construis entier,*
through all the experiences of others, of time, of nature. So
that Eluard can say, *Saisons passantes je suis...*, so that he
can also say that his *sang s'élève sur ses ruines.*
The employment of imagery is the process of reducing the
visible world to a fine powder, as the ore is crushed to remake,
from the elements, an enduring structure; in this structure, his
own inner vision is sensitized and the external world takes on
the purity of light. Critics frequently refer to this process as
poetic alchemy. In a way it is a search for the original world,
the *recherche de l'enfance perdue* of Rimbaud. But whereas
Rimbaud's world ended in flight, Eluard's world ends in a re-
statement of personal sincerity and moral integrity which lies
at the basis of his choice of imagery. Further, this world is
made one, integrated into a complete and whole statement. The
reader is reminded, in reading Eluard, of Baudelaire's appreciation of Hugo in *L'Art romantique*:

Victor Hugo was, from the beginning, the man best endowed, the most visibly chosen to express, through poetry, that which I will call the *mystery of life.* Nature which places before us, whichever way we turn, and which envelops us like a mystery, shows herself under several simultaneous states, each one of which, according to the extent it reacts in us, our intelligence and our sensitivity, is reflected more acutely in our hearts: form, attitude and movement, light and color, sound and harmony.[9]

In the eighteenth stanza of "Règnes" (*Le Livre ouvert,* I), for example, the reader can see a similar organization of materials into a single integrated view of reality:

> *Les fleurs les feuilles les épines*
> *Redevinrent visibles*
> *Les bourgeons et la rosée*
> *Virent le jour*
> *Sous le fleuve de mai*
> *Une voile écarlate*
> *Fit battre le pouls du vent*
> *Sous couleurs de vie et d'espace*
> *Sous forme de légers nuages*
> *Sans un frisson*
> *Le sein de l'aube consentait.*

(The flowers the leaves the thorns / Became visible again / The birds and the dew saw the day / Under the river of May / A scarlet sail / Caused the pulse of the wind to beat / Under the color of life and space / Under the form of light clouds / Without a shudder / The breast of the dawn gave its consent.)

The form of the verse reflects the flowing quality of the images of the poem (opening buds, flowers, rivers, clouds), which tend towards a fixed state reflected in the simple literary past tense of the verbs. The attitude towards these phenomena of the world is both acceptance of the image itself, the *don du poème,* as well as a simultaneous refusal to hold on to what is given, a kind of consent, as *le sein de l'aube consentait.* There is light: The entire poem has to do with light in all of its density (*jour,* the heavy light of *écarlate*) and opacity (*nuages*). The *harmonie du vers* is apparent: the repetition of the consonants *f* and *v.*

The poem expresses through such a combination, as Baudelaire finds in Hugo, *le mystère de la vie*, which is the secret of Eluard's understanding of the reality of the world as he brings it over into the poem and redefines both the unwilling from his subconscious and also the image reticent to be captured, in a very moving statement of the necessity of acknowledging the real. And from this acknowledgment, Eluard can proceed to an understanding of his own solitude and how this understanding makes the real more meaningful. The way is one of images; the functioning of the images, in turn, makes possible a constant awareness of both oneself and the world.

CHAPTER 3

Reality of Experience: the Theory of Love

I *The Experience of Love*

ELUARD is perhaps best known as a love poet. Love, as a central theme of Eluard's poetry, becomes especially evident around 1923; yet, throughout his poetic career Eluard wrote poems about the experiences one has in being with another person, loving that person, and being without that person. He further expanded his individual involvement to involvement with humanity, the experiences one has in being with people, wanting to do something for others so that happiness and fulfillment might result. More profoundly, this experience is a way of acknowledging his own solitude and deepening his own poetic awareness. It is as a love poet, then, that he reaches the most precise appreciation of reality and achieves a total statement of the two realities of the self and the outside world.

In the title of a book of poems in his early period, Eluard states his doctrine of love: *Mourir de ne pas mourir*. The title helps the reader to understand the nature of the problem of love in Eluard. As death is defined in terms of absence, dying is a result of not dying; therefore love is defined in terms of absence. Eluard is much more absolute, much more pure, than Baudelaire in his way of viewing love. For Eluard, the figure of the beloved invests all reality. In "L'Amoureuse" (*Mourir de ne pas mourir*) she is present not only physically, but also becomes one with the lover through their reciprocal awareness of each other's love: *Elle a la forme de mes mains / Elle a la couleur de mes yeux* ("She has the shape of my hands, / She has the color of my eyes"). The experience of love is thus, for Eluard, a total one: There are never two separate experiences (as in Proust), but a union of the beloved and the person in love, yet the loneliness remains a constant point of reference from which to seek identity with the other person. Love, for Eluard, is related to the subconscious experiments of the Surrealists. Love is not calculated, but derives from the inner recesses of the subconscious; it has, therefore, an immediacy. The notion of love is that of constant preoccupation (*Elle . . . ne me laisse pas dormir*, "She does not let me sleep"); the effect of love is a madness with no other cause than itself (*Ses rêves . . . me font . . Parler sans avoir rien à dire*, "Her dreams . . . make me . . . Speak without having anything to say"). It is the equivalence of love with madness that brings Eluard into the tradition of love from the Middle Ages on, the tradition of Iseult and Tristan.

The experience of love is also close to the experience of death: *Pour me trouver des raisons de vivre, j'ai tenté de détruire mes raisons de t'aimer* ("In order to find reasons for living, I tried to destroy my reasons for loving you"), Eluard writes in "Nuits partagées" (*La Vie immédiate*). Love is unreasonable and leads to madness (*folie*), much like *la folie de Tristan: Pour me trouver des raisons de t'aimer, j'ai mal vécu*, "In order to find reasons for living, I misspent my life" ("Nuits partagées," *La Vie immédiate*). The association of madness, on both the controlled (poetic) level (similar to Rimbaud's *dérèglement de tous les sens*) and on the emotional level, relates Eluard's view to that of other writers on love in the twentieth century. Like Proust, Eluard sees love as the temporary abandonment of reason. Unlike Proust, the return of reason does not bring with it the loss of love. in "Comme deux gouttes d'eau" (*La Rose publique* [*The Public Rose*]), Eluard speaks of the range of love, of the wiles of love: *L'amour unique tendait tous les pièges du prisme* ("The single love spread all the snares of the prism").[1] Eluard further reinforces this notion of reason and unreason as the dual aspects of love: two springs (fountains) brought together (*Des sources mêlées à des sources*); light and dark, music and silence (*Un clavier de neige dans la nuit*); excitement and dullness (*Tour à tour frissonnant et monotone*); the balancing of actions, ending in an absolute inaction somewhat similar to Baudelaire's *acédie* (*Une fuite un retour nul n'était parti / Tout menait au tourment / Tout menait au repos*); the wrath of daily living and the calm of love (*De longs jours étoilés de colères / Pour de longs jours aux ternures de baiser*). Time itself

is weighted, the past vanishes and the future no longer exists
(*L'enfance à travers l'automne d'un instant / Pour épuiser
l'avenir*).

Inherent in Eluard's viewpoint is a Platonism (already evident before *Mourir de ne pas mourir*) which derives from the
duality of his experiences. The earlier dualism maintains a balance between a general accidence of the moment and time contrasted with the general notion of being. For a Platonic poet,
an extension of this concept holds that the result of knowledge
from accidence is inferior to the knowledge obtained from
contemplation of being (or pure Form). This dualism poses a
problem that, in the estate of love, the accidence of the situation
in which the relationship operates must lead—if it is to have
meaning—to attaining a vision of the underlying essence of Form.
Eluard's evaluation of the experience of love is chiefly Platonic,
in that it does lead to a kind of contemplation of Form which
is transferred, in turn, to the reflected form which is the poem.
Yet Eluard, being a poet and not a philosopher or a meta-
physician, would never deny the continued need of the acci-
dental situation, which is the only one he can actually deal with
if he is to remain a poet. For Eluard, the value of experience
is that it is useful as a way of knowledge. In the ethical pro-
gram of Eluard, which is completely secular, the search for
knowledge does not end with the greater love of God as the
purpose of all action. Eluard would contend that the meaning
of all that happens to a person is found in the experience of
having loved another. For example, Eluard takes the commonplace image of the eyes of the beloved, the image that extends
from *amour courtois* through Petrarch and through the Renaissance, and qualifies the image of the eyes with the adjective
fertiles:

> *Tes yeux.* . . .
> *Ont fait à mes lumières d'homme*
> *Un sort meilleur qu'aux nuits du monde.*
> ("On ne peut me connaître," *Les Yeux fertiles*)

(Your eyes. . . . / Have made of my lights as a man / A better
fate than the nights of the world.)

The interest is ethical, the experience is expanded to include the common good, not only the good of the person involved in the particular experience with one other person. The eyes that betray the love the other person has for him also imply a principle of knowledge; this knowledge retains a meaning which is again both natural and naturalistic in tone and intent:

> *Tes yeux dans lesquels je voyage*
> *Ont donné aux gestes des routes*
> *Un sens détaché de la terre. (Ibid.)*

(Your eyes in which I travel / Have given to the gestures of the ways / A sense cut off from earth.)

Eluard finds difficulty in reconciling a search for a higher good with an experience which must be resolved by attributing another meaning to the love experience than contemplation, especially contemplation of the significance of his own aloneness and the uniqueness of his perceptions. This dilemma is to be expressed in terms of the poetry within which he works—the subconscious, the power of the word, the organically organized image. The meaning of love, though physical and secular, is brought into a higher focus of the world at large; the meaning of the world brings in an additional entanglement of all that would prevent clarity of view. In a way, the meaning of love is an inversion of the religious experience. In the dark night of the world, the principle of love gives meaning and significance; the light of the world is the light of the beloved's eyes. In accordance with Eluard's principle of humanitarian concerns, the knowledge of the true meaning of the world which the light of the beloved's eyes reveals also reveals the meaning of the actions of others:[2]

> *Dans tes yeux ceux qui nous révèlent*
> *Notre solitude infinie*
> *Ne sont plus ce qu'ils croyaient être. (Ibid.)*

(In your eyes those who reveal to us / Our infinite solitude / Are no longer that which they believed themselves to be.)

This knowledge then gives significance to the woman he loves. The poem ends not with the woman's knowledge of the poet, but his knowledge of the woman:

> On ne peut pas te connaître
> Mieux que je te connais. (Ibid.)

(You cannot be known / Better than I know you.)

It is this invasion of the world by the knowledge of love that informs the world. The visual intent of Eluard requires that, as a poet, he see the world in the sense of images: *poesis*, or writing the poem, is the living quality, the making alive, of these images. It is love that rescues his poems from being merely photography of images or saves them from being merely sculpted or painted (as in much nineteenth-century poetry):

> Si tu aimes l'intense nue
> Infuse à toutes les images
> Son sang d'été. . . . ("Si tu aimes," Le Livre ouvert, II)[3]

(If you love the intense cloud / Infused in all the images / Its summer blood.)

As in the experience of love, opposites are brought together, so the knowledge gained through creating poetry, in light of the experience of love, brings together opposites in nature; this experience endows the poem with magic (*magie*) because of their function as correspondances in the manner of Baudelaire:

> Pour ce que tu veux rapprocher
> Allume l'aube dans la source
> Tes mains lieuses
> Peuvent unir lumière et cendre
> Mer et montagne
> Mâle et femelle neige et fièvre. (Ibid.)

(For that which you wish to bring together / Lights the dawn in the well-spring / Your hands that bind / Can unite light and ash / Sea and mountain / Male and female snow and fever.)

In asserting the love ethic operative throughout the universe, Eluard not only associates this ethic with an aesthetic principle of poetry and humanitarian interests, but also uses it as a description of his desire to deal with his private anguish and sense of apartness:

> *Et le nuage le plus vague*
> *La parole la plus banale*
> *L'objet perdu*
> *Force-les à battre des ailes*
> *Rends-les sensibles à ton coeur*
> *Fais-les servir la vie entière. (Ibid.)*

(And the most indefinite cloud / The commonest word / The lost object / Force them to beat their wings / Make them sensitive to your heart / Make them serve the whole of life.)

Without the presence of love the whole world loses its meaning:

Le soleil des champs croupit
Les soleil des bois s'endort
Le ciel vivant disparaît
Et le soir pèse partout ("Sans toi," *Le lit la table* [*The Bed the Table*])

(The sun of the fields stagnates / The sun of the woods fall asleep / The living sky disappears / And the evening weighs upon everything everywhere.)

Further, the dark night of despair will come:

> *Viendra la nuit la fin*
> *L'inhumaine nuit des nuits*
> *. . .*
> *Une nuit sans insomnie*
> *Sans un souvenir du jour. (Ibid.)*

(The weight of the end will come / The inhuman night of nights / . . . A night without sleepnessness / Without a memory of the day.)

Death will come and the loss of hope; without the presence of love there is no incentive to action:

> *La mort ni simple ni double*
> *Vers la fin de cette nuit*
> *Car nul espoir n'est permis*
> *Car je risque plus rien.* (*Ibid.*)

(Death neither single nor double / Towards the end of this night /
For no hope is allowed / For I risk nothing any more.)

The incentive to action, which is one way of dealing with solitude, is not the only apology for love in Eluard. He finds in it
repose, tenderness, *la tendresse de la nuit.* In contrast to the
anguish and distress which Baudelaire frequently encounters
in the relationship, in contrast to the sadism of the *Fleurs du mal,*
Eluard finds a quiet pleasure:

> *Rose à finir sous les lèvres*
> *En silence sous les lèvres*
> *Du plus grand plaisir connu.* ("Repos d'été")[4]

(Rose which ends beneath the lips / In silence beneath the lips /
Of the greatest pleasure known.

Eluard is close to the Romantic tradition of a poetry of daily
life, *la poésie de la vie quotidienne: le jour coule dans la rue*
("the day flows in the street"). Eluard, however, extends and
deepens the theme through his awareness both of the physical
awareness of the woman and of the poet's solitude:

> *Tous inspirés tous absents*
> *Tous faisant face au désert.* (*Ibid.*)

(All those inspired all those absent / All those facing the desert.)

He glances at a garden and finds a temporal hope: *Terre terre
espoir et terre....* (Earth earth hope and earth") and the experience of beauty:

> *Sous les gerbes et les arcs*
> *Fuit une foule de grains*
> *Fuit la flamme et la fraîcheur*
> *Pour un seul épi modèle*
> *Plus fort que le ciel lointain.* (*Ibid.*)

(Under the sheaves and the bows / Flees a crowd of grains / Flees the flame and the coolness / For a single model ear of corn / Stronger than the distant sky.)

Love has the power to destroy time understood in the sense of a measurable time; love leaves behind only a pure, absolute time and raises poetry to a level of meaning that is significant beyond the moment:

> *Toi première et dernière tu n'as pas vieilli*
> *Et pour illuminer mon amour et ma vie*
> *Tu conserves ton coeur de belle femme nue.*
> ("Pour un anniversaire")[5]

(You first and last you have not grown old / And to illuminate my life / You keep your heart of a beautiful nude woman.)

II Love as Meaning

More than illuminating life and giving meaning to the acts of those around him, emotions furnish the stuff or substance around which the poet weaves his poems: *ma mémoire est un fruit savoureux*, "my memory is a sweet fruit" ("Seule"). His evaluation includes the sterility and silence of the love relationship as well as the fulfillment: *Mémoire et même du désert et du silence*, "Memory and even of the desert and the silence" ("Seule"). As in Mallarmé, images signify the absence of life: *Joli désert où la mort est légion*, "Pretty desert where death is legion" ("Seule"). For Eluard, when the emotions cannot work effectively, time brings nihilism: *Le coeur parcelle et le temps dispersion*, "the heart a particle time a dispersion" ("Seule"). Once more the anguish of the dark night is evident when no clear meaning is possible: *Silence noir où tout se contredit*, "Black silence where everything is contradicted" ("Seule"). Then the eyes of the women cause him to laugh and sing. The poet's solitude, as a result, is overcome and he is able to say: *Le jour bâillonne le silence*, "Day gags the silence" ("Seule").

Eluard describes moments when time overflows: *Le Temps déborde* (*Time Overflows*) is the title of a late collection of poems. In "L'Extase" he describes similar moments of poetic delirium.[6] The opening lines are reminiscent of Baudelaire: *Je suis devant ce paysage féminin / Comme un enfant devant le feu* ("I am before this feminine landscape / Like a child before the fire"). The notion of a woman as a landscape (*paysage*) is common to both Eluard and Baudelaire. Love is a visual exploration in both poets. "L'Extase" can be read as an explanation of the ethic of love. The emotion expressed is one of tenderness and comfort and is domestic in tone as a child before the fire, *souriant vaguement et les larmes aux yeux*. Love has the power to move; it is a dialectic of two conditions, dark and light, of two contrasting seasons:

> *Devant ce paysage où tout se remue en moi*
> *Où des miroirs s'embuent où des miroirs s'éclairent*
> *Reflétant deux corps nus saison contre saison.* ("L'Extase")

(In front of this landscape where in all stirs in me / Wherein mirrors grow clearer / Reflecting two nude bodies season against season.)

As in Baudelaire, the dialectic endows experience with movement, avoids a kind of stasis. But Eluard, unlike Baudelaire, tries to reconcile the two conditions. Further, love is also a loss of self, an unknown voyage, a means of knowledge; eventually possession occurs in the sense that the poet takes on the nature of the woman he loves:

> *J'ai tant de raisons de me perdre*
> *Sur cette terre sans chemins et sous ce ciel sans horizon*
> *Belles raisons que j'ignorais hier*
> *Et que je n'oublierai jamais*
> *Belles clés des regards clés filles d'elles-mêmes*
> *Devant ce paysage féminin.* (*Ibid.*)

(I have so many reasons for losing myself / Upon this earth without roads and under this sky without horizon / Beautiful reasons that I did not know yesterday / And that I shall never forget / Beautiful keys of glances daughters of themselves / In front of this landscape where nature belongs to me.)

In love Eluard would seek the origin of life, the very beginnings of his existence which make him unique and alone; it is a place of origin where all that is within him and outside him have become reconciled:

> *Devant le feu le premier feu*
> *Bonne raison maîtresse*
> *Etoile identifiée*
> *Et sur la terre et sous le ciel de mon coeur et dans mon coeur*
> *Second bourgeon première feuille verte*
> *Que la mer couvre de ses ailes*
> *Et le soleil au bout de tout venant de nous.* (*Ibid.*)

(Before the fire the first fire / Good reason mistress / Star identified / And on the earth and beneath the sky of my love and in my love / Second bud green leaf / That the sea covers with its wings / And the sun at the end of everything coming from us.)

The final act of love is one consummation, as in the fire the phoenix dies to be reborn (Eluard has given the title *Le Phénix* to one of his books): *Je suis devant ce paysage féminin / Comme une brande dans le feu.*

Love is always the metaphysical center of Eluard's poetry, love in the sense of reconciliation of opposites, despair and desire, spirit and flesh, the self of solitude and the self of alienation. In the "spectacle" of the day-to-day experience of love (which is the basis of Eluard's discussion of love), a "supernatural" condition prevails. This condition is "above" the experience; it endows the experience—however prosaic in one way —with a quality close to poetic inspiration because of the fusion of opposites. Awareness of this fusion becomes the occasion of a poem. Such an occasion is very close to Baudelaire's definition of the symbol:

In certain states of the soul, which are almost supernatural, the profoundness of life is shown quite completely in the sight (*spectacle*), however commonplace, which is before one's eyes. This sight becomes the symbol of that profoundness.[7]

The emphasis in these lines is on the verb "becomes." It supports a theory of poetry which underlies Eluard's work. The poem, even though it refers to an event which could be taken in an anecdotal sense, still maintains a wider horizon, a deeper vision of reality, because it has taken on a symbolic meaning;

it has become gesture, act, a coming together in the etymological sense of the word symbol. Baudelaire has defined similar privileged moments of poetry in *Fusées*: "There are moments of existence when time and extension are deeper, and the feeling of existence is immensely increased."[8]

The experience of love, as it becomes the poem, seems to occur at a distance, as though the poet in his solitude had separated himself from the woman he loves and was looking at love from a distance, as though something tremendous and overpowering and awesome had happened. This experience possesses such qualities because Eluard sees himself not only as a man in love and a poet writing about love, but also as a man. It is the force that binds his poetry together into an organic whole, that causes his images and his ideas to grow and come forth as shoots in the spring. Love, for Eluard, is always present; it dominates his loneliness, and even when absent from the woman he loves, he is possessed by love. Yet it is not the love of *la princesse lointaine* of medieval lyricism. Eluard does not submit himself to love as ritual (which is frequently true of Baudelaire). Rather, Eluard seeks to be more aware of love as the metaphysical center of his universe and his being.

In all of his poetic career, Eluard is preoccupied with exploration of this metaphysic. In the poem "Première du monde" (*Capitale de la douleur*), Eluard speaks of the woman as a universal, as the first woman in the world.[9] He attempts to see his individual love as a manifestation of a universal idea. The woman is described as a being possessed by earth (*captive de la plaine*) and—at the same time—possessed by spirit (*agonisante folle*). Light hides itself in her (*la lumière sur toi se cache*); the poet tells her to look at the sky and the sky attacks her dreams (*s'en prendre à ton rêve*), possibly to awaken her to light. The sky closes her dress in order to break her chains so that the light of the sky might break her bondage. In other words, the freedom which woman, in general, possesses can be broken only by blind force and darkness.

III *Poetic Vision and the Statement of Experience*

Eluard undergoes, in moments of poetic vision, an experience which corresponds to that of meditation and, in particular, poetic meditation. His view of poetic meditation is close to Hugo's discussion of the *vates*:

> The extent of the possible is in some way beneath your eyes. The dream you have in yourself, you find outside yourself. All is indistinct. ... From all sides the various densities of effects and causes. ... We have only the choice of the dark. ... You become a *vates*. A vast religious meditation takes hold of you.[10]

In "Première du monde," Eluard describes the visionary ends of poetry in the mystery of woman. These ends are similar in intent to those described by Hugo when he speaks of the poet seer finding his way through darkness and obscurity. In the view of both poets, a personal vision is joined to a poetic vision.

In the second stanza of "Première du monde," Eluard describes the power of woman: She is a complex of wheels, perhaps in reference to the mandala and the symbol of birth and eternal rebirth, *Devant toutes les roues nouées*. She has the power, by her seductiveness and sensuality, to attract man, *Un éventail rit aux éclats*. She is described as "grass," wherein man becomes lost, *Dan les traîtres filets de l'herbe*; as the place where roads (direction, purpose, meaning) lose their *reflets* (the ability to give meaning to life). Implicit in these lines is the eternal struggle or drama between man and woman, between light and dark. In a way, the poet's struggle is a masculine protest against the overwhelming power of woman and love. Eluard then asks her what her capacity is and what she can do:

> *Ne peux-tu donc prendre les vagues*
> *Dont les barques sont les amandes*
> *Dans ta paume chaude et câline*
> *Ou dans les boucles de ta tête?*

(Can you not then take the waves / Whose boats are almonds / In your hot and caressing palm / Or in the curls of your head?)

He also asks her if she can grasp the stars. He speaks of her as *écartelée*, spread out in torture on a wheel (a sexual image). She resembles the stars; the poet sees her as she takes upon herself the maze of fire, *dans leur nid de feu tu demeures*. Her spendor is multiplied by it, *ton éclat s'en multiplie*.

In the fifth stanza of the same poem, Eluard speaks of the dawn as "gagged." The night is over and the dawn is struggling against the sun. A single cry is heard: The woman wishes to be possessed by love just as the sun tries to emerge from underneath the bark of a tree. The final stanza culminates the discussion or exploration of all the varied aspects of the love experience summed up in an affirmation of life: *O douce, quand tu dors, la nuit se mêle au jour* ("O my beloved, when you sleep, night is mixed with day"). The metaphysics of love, which is universal (the references to sky, stars, sun), the eternalization of the dramatic struggle between man and woman, is resolved in the union of man and woman. I believe that Eluard tries to present the drama of physical love from a psychic, almost Jungian, point of view. He wishes to transform the woman from nonlight to light. In the tension of the poem, the woman remains in the eternal position of woman, an enigma of opposites.

The significance of this transformation lies in the poet's continued attempt to define and to live with his individual solitude, his fundamental loneliness. He sees in this enigma a reflection of his own duality, his own idea of himself, caught between a necessary solitude and an equally necessary participation in the life of another. His own existence, the fact even of existing, is definable only as a dilemma. Eluard further explores the dilemma, which is most apparent in a notion of love, in the final poem of *Capitale de la douleur*, entitled "Celle de toujours, toute." He describes not only the physical presence of woman, as in "Première du monde," but also the absence of woman, or the nonfeminine principle. He has given up all, for the woman absorbs, one might say, the man:

> *Si je vous dis: "j'ai tout abandonné"*
> *C'est qu'elle n'est pas celle de mon corps.*

(If I say that I have given up everything / It is that she is not the woman of my body.)

He has passed through the carnal experience as through a fog:

> *Et la brume de fond où je me meus*
> *Ne sait jamais si j'ai passé.*

(And the inner fog where I move / Never knows when I have passed by.)

In the second stanza of "Celle de toujours, toute," Eluard further elaborates on the experience of love. Love is like a mirror through which the poet passes:

> *L'éventail de sa bouche, le reflet de ses yeux*
> *Je suis le seul à en parler,*
> *Je suis le seul qui soit cerné*
> *Par ce miroir si nul où l'air circule à travers moi.*

(The fan of her mouth, the reflection of light of her eyes / I am the only one to speak of them / I am the only one who is held in by it / By this mirror, so nonexistent, where the air circulates through me.)

In contrast to the self, the *moi*, surrounded by the mirror, he defines the presence of woman as participating in a larger scheme of natural phenomena:

> *Et l'air a un visage, un visage aimé,*
> *Un visage aimant, ton visage,*
> *A toi qui n'as pas de nom et que les autres ignorent,*
> *La mer te dit: sur moi, le ciel te dit: sur moi,*
> *Les astres te devinent, les nuages t'imaginent.*

(And the air has a face, a beloved face / A loving face, your face, / To you, the one who is nameless and whom the others do not know, / The sea says to you: on me, the sky says to you: on me, / The heavenly bodies predict you, the clouds imagine you.)

The woman is thus perceived as more universal than man; she has the gift of understanding the life-force:

> *Et le sang répandu aux meilleurs moments,*
> *Le sang de la générosité*
> *Te porte avec délices.*

(And the blood spilt at the best moments, / The blood of generosity / Bears you with delight.)

The final stanza of "Celle de toujours, toute," defines the poet's role; it also defines the male role, as apart from the woman's, as well:

> Je chant la grande joie de te chanter,
> La grande joie de t'avoir ou de ne pas t'avoir,
> La candeur de t'attendre, l'innocence de te connaître

(I sing the great joy of singing of you, / The great joy of having you or not having you, / The candor of waiting for you, the innocence of knowing you.)

Woman has the power to suppress oblivion (hope, ignorance, absence); woman has brought man into the world: *O toi qui supprimes l'oubli, l'espoir et l'ignorance, / Qui supprimes l'absence et qui me mets au monde.* The mystery of woman is to bring love into the world in the act of creation, so the act of loving woman is the poet's freedom. The principle of creativity is purer than the instrument:

> Je chante pour chanter, je t'aime pour chanter
> Le mystère où l'amour me crée et se délivre.
> Tu es pure, tu es encore plus pure que moi-même.

(I sing in order to sing, I love you in order to sing / The mystery where love creates me and delivers me. / You are pure, even purer than I myself.)

For Eluard love is the source of creativity. The inspiration from love is enlarged beyond the Renaissance or Romantic concept and made more profound. The sixteenth century developed two notions of love, naturalism and mysticism, both of which grew out of medieval ideas of courtly love and humanist studies of 'Neoplatonism. Both notions are found in Eluard; yet his mysticism is far less intellectualized and more deeply felt and his naturalism more spontaneous and freer in movement than in sixteenth-century poetry. His verse, moreover, has less Byronic a pose than has nineteenth-century poetry. The inspiration, in a given poem, derives from a love that goes beyond the mere occasion of the poem. Eluard gives inspiration a more ethical tone; his incentive for writing verse is, in effect, a fulfilling of the self, a realization of the fullest possible meaning of his solitude. This solitude is further defined as a source of creativity. Again a dilemma is operative, for, in creating poetry, the poet fulfills the role of woman in his life; at the same time, he fulfills his own creativity. His own power to create is thus realized:

> *Je n'ai rien séparé mais j'ai doublé mon coeur,*
> *D'aimer, j'ai tout créé: réel, imaginaire,*
> *J'ai donné sa raison, sa forme, sa chaleur*
> *Et son rôle immortel à celle qui m'éclaire.*
>
> ("En vertu de l'amour," *Le Temps déborde*)[11]

(I have separated nothing but I have doubled my heart, / From loving I have created everything: real, imaginary, / I gave its reason, its shape, its warmth / And its immortal role to the woman who brings me light.)

This realization is the strength of love. It is concerned with death and with the conquering of death. Without love, life is silence: *Masque de neige sur la terre et sous la terre / Source des larmes dans la nuit masque d'aveugle,* "Mask of snow on the earth and under the earth / Source of tears in the night mask of a blind man" ("Notre vie," *Le Temps déborde*).[12]

Love is the force of life. In "Dit de la force de l'amour,"[13] the force of love is placed against injustice and misfortune, *l'injustice et ce malheur des hommes.* Love, then, is the force that brings and continues freedom. The idea is one of a continued organic function of life, similar to the organic structure of the images of love in poetry. The woman, who gave back freedom to man, stands for the freedom that the world will one day give back to man:

> *Toi qui fus de ma chair la conscience sensible*
> *Toi que j'aime à jamais toi qui m'as inventé*
> *Tu ne supportais pas l'oppression ni l'injure*
> *Tu chantais en rêvant le bonheur sur la terre*
> *Tu rêvais d'être libre et je te continue.*
>
> ("Dit de la force de l'amour")

(You who were of my flesh the sensitive awareness / You whom I love forever you who invented me / You did not bear either opposition or insult / You sang as you dreamed of happiness on earth / You dreamed of being free and I prolong your dream.)

For Eluard this gift of liberty is the eternal presence of love: *Le présent, c'est mon coeur. Le rythme de mon coeur est un rythme éternel* ("Les Sentiers et les routes de la poésie").[14] Eluard defines this presence in "Dominique aujourd'hui présente" (*Le Phénix*):

> *O toi mon agitée et ma calme pensée*
> *Mon silence sonore et mon écho secret*
> *Mon aveugle voyante et ma vue dépassée*
> *Je n'ai plus eu que ta présence*
> *Tu m'as couvert de ta confiance.*

(O you my troubled and my quiet thought / My sonorous silence and my secret echo / My blind one who sees and my sight that goes beyond / I had nothing else than your presence / You covered me with your confidence.)

In the poem "La Mort l'amour la vie" (*Le Phénix*), the love of woman is described as universal, embracing all mankind. The poet perceives his own solitude:

> *J'ai cru pouvoir briser la profondeur l'immensité*
> *Par mon chagrin tout nu sans contact sans écho*
> *Je me suis étendu dans ma prison aux portes vierges*
> *Comme un mort raisonnable qui a su mourir*
> *Un mort non couronné sinon de son néant*
> *Je me suis étendu sur les vagues absurdes*
> *Du poison absorbé par mon amour la cendre*
> *La solitude m'a semblé plus vive que le sang.*

(I thought that I had been able to shatter depth immensity / By my unhappiness all bare without contact without echo / I lay down in my prison with its virgin gates / Like a reasonable dead man who has learned how to die / A man dead not crowned unless by his nothingness / I lay down on the absurd waves / Of the poison absorbed by love the ash / The aloneness seemed to me more alive than blood.)

In this solitude, he wishes for annihilation: *J'avais éliminé l'hivernale ossature / Du voeu de vivre qui s'annule* ("I had eliminated the winter's skeleton / From the desire to live which dies"). Although Eluard is aware of love as a form of death, or as a death-wish following the medieval tradition of Iseult and Tristan, he strives to equate love with life. The woman arrives, through her loneliness is vanquished, *Tu es venue la solitude est vaincue*; he has found a way in life, *J'avais un guide sur la terre* ("L'Amour la mort la vie"). Fear is dissipated and all seems new and fresh:

> *Les rayons de tes bras entr'ouvraient le brouillard*
> *Ta bouche était mouillée des premières rosées*
> *Le repos ébloui remplaçait la fatigue*
> *Et j'adorais l'amour comme à mes premiers jours.*

(The rays of your arms half opened the mist / Your mouth was wet with the first dews / The dazzled repose replaced the tiredness / And I adored love as in my first days.)

Eluard extends the visionary quality of the love experience to include all life:

> *Les champs sont labourés les usines rayonnent*
> *Et le blé fait son nid dans une houle énorme*
> *La moisson la vendange ont des témoins sans nombre.*

(The fields are plowed the factories shine / And the wheat makes its nest in an enormous surge / The harvest and the grape-gathering have innumerable witnesses.)

This vision has always been a part of Eluard's belief. The first part of the poem "Nous sommes" (*Chanson complète*), although terminating on a sombre note, shows the universality of woman, all that she sees (*tu vois*): the fire, the sea. He then lists precise objects: stones, sidewalks, a public square, a house; then animals, then birds. In the stanza following the categories, Eluard describes woman through the symbol of the mirror: the woman who brings forth youth, faith, light:

Des femmes descendant de leur ancien miroir
T'apportant leur jeunesse et leur foi en la tienne
Et l'une sa clarté la voile qui t'entraîne
Te fait secrètement voir le monde sans toi.

(Women coming down from their ancient mirror / Bring to you their faith in yours / And the one her transparency the veil which carries you along / Makes you see, secretly, the world without you.)

The vision is enlarged to include all men. The light of love, the illumination given by love, enables men, who are at first workers in the field, to become dreamers and hence poets. And the poets are those who go "gathering their dreams" (*vont cueillir tous leurs songes*), those whom the poet sees "sleeping from delight in the sound of the sun" (*dormir de joie au bruit du soleil*). In "Les Sept poèmes d'amour en guerre" (*Au Rendez-vous allemand* [*At the German Meetingplace*]), Eluard speaks of the eyes of love in terms of a past experience: *Patients tes yeux nous attendaient*. He then describes them in terms of life and growth:

Ils étaient une vallée
Plus tendre qu'un seul brin d'herbe
Leur soleil donnait du poids
Aux maigres moissons humaines
Nous attendaient pour nous voir
Toujours
Car nous apportions de l'amour
La jeunesse de l'amour
Et la raison de l'amour
La sagesse de l'amour
Et l'immortalité

(They were a valley / More tender than a single blade of grass / Their sun gave weight to the thin human harvests / Waited for us to see one another / For we bore love / The youth of love / And the reason of love / The wisdom of love / And the immortality.)

Parallel to the poet's captivity and solitude is the captivity of the nation. He finds in this captivity truth which would serve as a refuge (*qui nous servait d'asile*). Eluard believes in the eventual triumph of love.

Of all the experiences which are the subjects of poetry, the one which is constantly present is that of love, because it is the experience in light of which the poet examines most precisely his own solitude. His aloneness becomes most apparent when he is faced by another person, who also lives a present situation of solitude. It is this experience that frees him, not so much from solitude itself, as from the anguish of solitude. Frequently Eluard expands specific considerations of the nature and function of love into a kind of metaphysics. For example, in accordance with Surrealist doctrine, the goal of art is the total emancipation of man. Love is essentially the freeing of man so that he may understand the captivity in which he lives. Woman represents for Eluard the welding of opposites: She is the fog, the sea, the mystery of darkness. She is also light, the sun, the paths. The reconciliation of these opposites constitutes the poet's role and is the reason which informs his work. From this role and this reason derives also the poet's attempt to teach a reader the possibility of this reconciliation. Because it brings together two ways of seeing reality and thus meaning, it points the way towards creativity in the private life of the individual reader. From this creativity, in turn, comes freedom for man. Thus the reality of loves exists for Eluard. Life is an immediacy, especially an immediacy of solitude, most evident in the experience of love. And, paradoxically, because of love, this solitude brings men together.

CHAPTER 4

Reality of the Mind: the Surrealist Ideal

I Eluard and the Search for the Absolute

THE basic problem in Surrealist poetry is that of knowledge, and more particularly, that of intuition. Eluard deepens the import of this problem because, from his private solitude and anguish, he wishes to discover a world of absolute meaning. Quite possibly this world is one of dream and objects to which he must attribute meaning that is both personal and absolute. He confronts the question of evocation, of calling up from the dream world those associations which give meaning to the poetic experience. The difficulty is how to define the poetic state, the extent to which the poet's intuition partakes of the existence of the object, and to show how the poet grasps the essential nature of the object. The poet reveals how he comes to know that the object exists and how his comprehension of it evolves. His intuitive knowledge is close to the dream state, as Valéry pointed out in "Poésie et pensée abstraite":

The poetic universe offers great analogies with that which we can suppose of the universe of dream. . . . our memories of dreams teach us, by a common and frequent experience, that our consciousness can be overrun, filled, entirely saturated by the output of an existence (la production d'une existence), the objects and beings of which appear the same as those in the waking state; but their meanings, their relationships and their modes of variation and substitution are quite different and doubtlessly represent to us, as do symbols of allegories, the immediate fluctuations of our general sensibility, which is not controlled by the sensibilities of our specialized senses. It is more or less in this manner that the poetic state is set up, develops, and finally is separated from us.[1]

Valéry's point is that the poet's consciousness is saturated by the production d'une existence. In Donner à voir (Gift of Vision),

70

Eluard writes of the "Juste milieu," an attempt to take hold precisely of the *production d'une existence*: This poem represents a kind of saturation resulting from a process of poetic knowledge, or more exactly, in the poetic production of that existence.

In "Crépuscule," the first part of the prose poems which make up "Juste milieu," Eluard describes his knowledge of twilight. The first lines concern those associations and actions which give the reader the tone of the twilight. The effect is neither plastic nor painterly; these lines reproduce the state of the poet's mind and his free associations:

> *Désert vertical, le verrier creusait la terre,*
> *le fossoyeur voulait se pendre et dans la fumée,*
> *de ma tête s'organisait l'oubli.*

(Vertical descent, the glassmaker dug the earth, the gravedigger wanted to hang himself and in the smoke of my head forgetfulness became organized.)

The method in these lines is a combination of free association with the conscious notation of a state of mind. The poet pushes himself forward from this state into the existence of the objects contemplated which surround him. He is trying, moreover, to bring the exactness of the object into his awakened mind. The poetic point of view is towards the past and the total recall of events and emotions of the past which are now a part of his solitude and which he can now, in some measure, relive. In "Crépuscule," this recall consists of associations of twilight with images of burial and suicide, the poet's unwilling desire to forget the past and yet his equally strong wish to forget the past which is a kind of death of the past. The poet's forgetfulness of the past is associated with other images and thus gives him a knowledge of twilight at that moment. Eluard continues:

> *C'était l'heure entre chien et loup, entre suie*
> *et poix. Un joli vertige. Avant de disparaître,*
> *le ciel fit une grimace cornue. Je vivais, petit,*
> *tranquille, bien au chaud, car j'avais enchâssé*
> *ma précieuse ferveur diurne dans la dure poitrine de*
> *mes ennemis vaincus.*

(It was the hour between dog and wolf, between soot and pitch. A pretty dizziness. Before disappearing, the sky gave a crooked grimace. I lived, small, tranquil, very warm, because I had enshrined my precious divine fury in the hard chest of my vanquished enemies.)

Here the *modes de variation et de substitution*, in Valéry's terms, show the fluctuations of Eluard's general sensitivity. The actions of the glassmaker and the gravedigger of the first stanza are replaced or varied by the idea contained in the phrase *l'heure entre chien et loup*. This phrase shows the poet's malaise and his awareness of the impossibility of escape from twilight. Such modes are prefigured as symbols or allegories and are instances of specialized control by the intellect; they offer a general definition of the poet's mood which he describes as a *joli vertige*. The last line, then, emerges as a statement of the poet's feelings at the moment he is surrounded by the twilight (the hate which he cherishes for the enemy and which he throws back upon the enemy). Eluard's sensibility, however, has finally become "disintegrated" (*désagrégée*). Unlike Valéry, according to whose poetic principle the poet at this precise point takes over and views his experience objectively, literally as object, Eluard views his experience as concluded at this point because his knowledge is peculiarly intuitive.

The origin of poetic knowledge, for Eluard, lies in latent dream, which in a way is quite autonomous and most apparent in moments of being alone. Supervielle once wrote:

Poetry always comes to me in a latent dream. I am found of giving directions to this dream, except on days of inspiration when I have the impression that it is giving direction to itself all alone.

To dream is to forget the material nature of one's body, to merge in some way the outer world with the inner. I always dream a little what I see, even at the very moment, and the extent to which, I see.

But if I dream I am not the less attracted by a great precision, by a sort of hallucinated preciseness. Is it not in just this way that the dream of the person sleeping is made manifest? It is upon awakening that outlines are effaced and that the dream becomes soft, inconsistent . . .[2]

Also in the poem "Juste milieu," a part of the poem entitled "Yeux" can be construed as a statement of similar poetic principle. The poet is in a state of dream; his inspiration directs itself towards the object itself. His eyes merge with the sea in a sort of hallucinated preciseness (Supervielle's *exactitude hallucinée*):

> *Mes yeux, objets patients, étaient à jamais ouverts*
> *sur l'étendue des mers où je me noyais. Enfin une*
> *écume blanche passa sur le point noir qui fuyait.*
> *Tout s'effaça.*

(My eyes, patient objects, were forever opened upon the stretch of seas wherein I drowned. Finally a white spray went over the black, fleeing, point. Everything became blotted out.)

At the moment of conscious physical contact (*je me noyais*), the contours of the envisioned object fade away.

Behind such general considerations lies the pervasive influence of Hegel. Breton had become more and more interested in the German philosopher since the appearance of a brief quotation from Hegel in a passage by Nerval in the *First Manifesto*. In the *Second Manifesto*, Breton declared that the "Hegelian concept of the penetration of the exterior world into the subjective existence had remained uncontested."[3] The underlying attraction for the Surrealists of Hegel's idea lay in his notion of comprehending the Absolute.[4] In the quest for absolute experience, for the purest form of seeing, the Surrealists would search for a way of apprehending the Absolute, of discovering the Absolute as it resided in external sense-objects. The beauty of a poem should then emerge, for the Absolute would shine through after the experience. Most important of all, for the Surrealists and for Eluard, immediacy must be found in the object itself. The question is, then, how does a poet gain his knowledge so that he knows and recognizes the Absolute in it. More and more the Surrealists were preoccupied with this problem, as is apparent in Breton's *What Is Surrealism?*

Eluard's method of understanding the object, which is close to Hegel's understanding of the Absolute, is seen in the poem "Jardin perdu" (*Cours naturel*). The first stanza depicts a garden; Eluard tries at once to get at the concreteness of the garden as a whole:

Ce jardin donnait sur la mer
Gorge d'oeillet
Il imitait le bruit de l'eau
On sous-entendait la forêt.

(This garden looked out upon the sea / Throat of carnation / It imitated the sound of the water / One implied the forest.)

The details are primarily notes of the sensory qualifications of the experience; the method is association of the most intimate item of experience (*gorge d'oeillet*), which is visual, with the auditive, the experience most closely connected with the visual. The reader would expect the experience of the garden to continue to be visual; he is surprised that the "idealizational" statement should follow. Eluard has interrupted the expected association by underscoring another kind of sensuous experience. This quality of the unexpected nevertheless gives an interconnection to the poet's associations. Eluard thus attributes a tone of "absoluteness" to the experience and allows the beauty of the unexpected to shine through. Whether he is aware of it or not, Eluard follows Hegel's statement about "the superiority of the concrete over the abstract."

The following stanza of the poem "Jardin perdu" illustrates the Hegelian belief "in the inner unity of the contradictory conditions of phenomena":

Son coeur débitait l'air du large
En massifs calmes
Ses fleurs montaient à pas de feuilles
Vers les racines du jour tendre.

(Its heart split up the sea-air / Into calm mountains / Its flowers climbed with steps of leaves / Towards the roots of the tender light.)

At first glance, such Surrealist technique would appear to be simply ramblings of free-association. Yet the movement of the poem requires the tying together of the heart with the air (the inner and outer aspects); the flowers should go up (on their stalks, leaf by leaf) until they meet the day which thrusts down its light (the "roots" which the day sends down to the ground

and by which it ties itself to the ground and draws up water).
Again the reader finds the underlying notion of the unity and
interdependence of all living things, in accord with the "organic"
preoccupation of Eluard's poetics; it also reflects Eluard's profound concern with what means of unity, what kind of knowledge, exist between himself as he stands alone and the outside
world of objects and events. Once more the Hegelian definition
of knowledge as "the linking of the thought with the object" is
clear in the third stanza:

> *Ce jardin donnait sur la terre*
> *Ses caresses pesaient si peu*
> *Que des allées en jaillissaient*
> *D'elles-mêmes à chaque instant.*

(The garden looked out upon the earth / Its caresses weighed so
little / That paths sprang out from it / By themselves, at each
moment.)

The actual affection that Eluard derives from the experience of
the lost garden, the comfort that he gains in understanding the
unity of nature as well as his capacity to feel the object and to
satisfy simultaneously his quest for an "absolute knowledge"
are implied in the verse, *ses caresses pesaient si peu*. The verse is
also a valid statement of a garden perceived directly by a reader.
Eluard here follows the Surrealist inference from Hegel, as one
critic has pointed out:[5] "the true understanding of existence
depended on the knowledge of the interrelation of the subjective
with the objective, which in turn meant a refusal of the kind of
idealism that sought something finer than the concrete manifesta-
tions of reality." Such a refusal of the purely ideal, of making
the end of the poetic experience a perception in itself of an
abstraction, is reflected in the final stanza of "Jardin perdu":

> *Une gamme de perspectives*
> *S'offrait aux courants de la vue*
> *Et le soleil couleur d'avril*
> *Animait un ciel végétal.*

(A gamut of perspectives / Was offered to the streams of sight /
And the sun color of April / Animated a vegetal sky.)

The experience remains on the level of the sensory (*une gamme de perspectives, le soleil. . . . animait*); the reader can infer an abstract affirmation of a life principle. He must, however, as does the poet, remain on the visual level.

In other words, Eluard agrees with the Surrealist interpretation of Hegel's principle that an experience which seeks the Absolute must result from coming together in harmony of the mind and the object. For Eluard to write poetry is to "invent" objects; his poet's eye does not see their accustomed characteristics; he remakes the world in accordance with his solitary poetic vision. In one way, this process is an extension of the angelism of nineteenth-century poetry. The object could no longer be taken into the poet's self-created universe and function therein according to an assigned role. The object was separated from man; the poet's duty was to discover the "existence" of the object outside the one described by tradition. In another way, this process is a refutation of the Romantic tradition which called upon the object to support concepts of idealism and abstraction.

II   *Eluard's Criticism of the Object*

Throughout his career Eluard was preoccupied by the problem of the existence of the object. He tried to grasp the reality of the object by establishing a relationship between his inner self, his inner solitude, and the object. "Jardin perdu" offers an example of relationships between the concreteness of the object and the fluidity of the poet's inner psyche. The poem "Salvador Dali" (*La Vie immédiate*) offers a clearer example of the synthesis that both the poet and the painter attempted. Dali derived from the *scuola metafisica* of Chirico and Carrà, which emphasized not only metaphysical concerns, but also the painter's inner perceptiveness. He met Picasso in 1928, and later that same year, Desnos and Eluard. Dali's contribution to Surrealist doctrine is in his *paranoic-critical* method, which Dali defined as follows: "Paranoic-critical activity: spontaneous method of original knowledge based upon the interpretive-critical association of delirious phenomena."[6] With Dali this method turned out to be a sort of "image-interpretation" test: trying to see how many different animals in a cloud or a clump of trees. One critic has remarked: "Envisaged in this way, critical paranoia is not only a creative method in which we can easily recognize the 'means of forcing inspiration' and gazing at old walls advocated by Leonardo, but an attempt to disorganize the outside world, a sort of paroxysmal impetus towards disorientation."[7] Dali's activity implies a refashioning of the world to accord with the demands of the painter's own desire (which is not an outward "normal" state). I believe that Eluard tends to a similar disorientation of the world; unlike Dali, Eluard attempts to derive a statement of meaning from disorientation. Eluard, in his poetry, discredits the external world, as realistic objects; at the same time, he maintains the right of his psyche to discover and understand the truth of these objects.

The poem "Salvador Dali" consists of five stanzas beginning with the phrase *c'est en,* followed by the present participle; each stanza offers a series of equivalences, a simultaneity of action, as the grammatical construction indicates. The sixth stanza gives the reason for these equivalences (*c'est pour*); the final seventh stanza draws the conclusion. On the one hand, the poem presents the metaphysical notion of creativity; on the other, the faith in the objects in themselves, as they exist, apart from the poet.

In the first stanza Eluard speaks of the condition under which *le délie des sexes / Accroît les sentiments rugueux du père / En quête d'une végétation nouvelle* ("the thin line of the sexes / Increases the corrugated feelings of the father / In search of a new vegetation").[8] These states come about *en tirant les cordes des villes, en fanant les provinces* ("While pulling the cords of the cities, while putting the provinces in the sun"). The second stanza describes another state, *en lissant les graines imperceptibles des désirs* ("while polishing the imperceptible grains of desire"). The simultaneous action is that the *aiguille s'arrête complaisamment* ("the hand of the clock stops complacently"). The hand of the clock could be taken as the moment of time. The passage of time stops, and at this moment, all else pauses: *Sur la dernière minute de l'araignée et du pavot / Sur la céramique de l'iris et du point de suspension* ("Upon the last minute of the spider and the field-poppy / Upon the ceramic of the iris and upon the point of suspension"). At this moment,

moreover, there is a boldness of love which is like a lovers'
meeting at the railroad station: *Que l'aiguille se noue sur la
fausse audace / De l'arrêt dans les gares et du doigt de la pudeur*
("Let the hand be tied upon the false audacity / Of the stop
in the railroad stations and of the finger of modesty").
The third stanza has to do with parting: the music increases
(*le piano des mêlées des géants*, "The piano of the scuffles of
giants"); beauty is thus increased (*en pavant les rues de nids
d'oiseaux*, "by paving the streets with nests of birds"); hunger
is assuaged (*du profit de la famine*). The two people become
larger. The fourth stanza deals with artistic pleasure, faith in
the artist's material (*la bonne foi du métal*); the pleasurable
effect is similar to bouquets and other small objects one gathers
while staying in a village and puts in one's pockets (*au fond des
poches rayées de rouge*, "at the bottom of red-striped pockets").
The following stanza suggests the idea of fragility (*un rideau de
mouches*, "a curtain of flies"). There is also the notion of action
and involvement (a *pêcheuse malingre se défend des marins*, "a
malingering fisherwoman defends herself from the sailors").
The fisherwoman is not interested in the sea, in the idea of
absence, as would be the case in a poem by Mallarmé:

> *Le bois qui manque la forêt qui n'est pas là*
> *La rencontre qui n'a pas lieu.*

(The woods which lack the forest which is not there / The meeting
which does not take place.)

The lines, *la bouche qui n'est faite / Que pour pleurer une
arme* ("the mouth which is made only / To weep for a weapon"), indicate the idea that the weapon is the defense, the only
defense, against the presence of the table, the glass, the tears of
others. There is a metaphysics of the shadow (absence or partial
absence) which forges *le squelette du cristal de roche* ("the
skeleton of rock crystal"). We cannot really separate ourselves
from presence: *elle* (*la fille sans bijoux à la peau nue*, "the bare-
skinned girl without jewels") [*nous*] *tend ses bras nus* (she
stretches out her bare arms to us) in an attitude reminiscent
of Mallarmé's notion of pure beauty. The objects of life which
make up another presence are necessary, Eluard concludes:

> *Il faudrait bien par ci et par là des rochers des vagues*
> *Des femmes pour nous distraire pour nous habiller*
> *Ou des cerises d'émeraudes dans le lait de la rosée.*

(Here and there cliffs waves would be necessary / Women to distract us to dress us / Or cherries of emeralds in the milk of the dew.)

The problem still remains, however, of how to deal with the problem of absence and presence in terms of his own aloneness. He sees the problem in terms of the possibility of their coming together to form a totality, wherein both absence and presence can be maintained. Eluard then reviews the various instances when absence and presence fuse and coalesce: *tant d'aubes brèves dans les mains / Tant de gestes maniaques pour dissiper l'insomnie* ("so many brief dawns in the hands / So many crazy gestures to dissipate sleeplessness"). Eluard ends with an affirmation in the necessity of balance:

> *Face à l'escalier dont chaque marche est le plateau d'une balance*
> *Face aux oiseaux dressés contre les torrents*
> *L'étoile lourde du beau temps s'ouvre les veines.*

(Opposite the staircase each step of which is the pan of a scale / Opposite the birds set up against the torrents / The heavy star of good weather opens its veins.)

The reader perceives in the use of the object in these lines a principle described by one critic as "the destruction of the limits of space and gravity."[9] This principle has basically to do with knowledge and especially with Eluard's Platonism. He once wrote of reality as "the fight to the death with appearances" (*la lutte à mort avec les apparences*). In the world of the appearance of reality, Eluard seeks to discover the real truth and the real meaning of the object. Eluard writes further, in "Parfait" (*Répétitions*),[10] *Tout est enfin divisé / Tout se perd / Tout se brise et disparaît* ("Everything is finally divided / Everything becomes deformed and lost / Broken and disappears"). Starting from a tendency to remake the world, which is the way of Rimbaud and Mallarmé, and which is also a positive reaffirmation

of revolt and Dadaist nihilism, Eluard looks at the world about
him. His poetry is fluid, full of light and water and landscapes
that change and are modified. His poet's eye refuses, in accordance with the directive intelligence underneath the visual
act, to define the object solely in terms of the object itself following the realist manner of the late nineteenth century. He defines
the object in its potential to undergo division and redivision, to
be broken up into several component parts; this potential makes
possible the discovery of the hidden bond (*lien*) which exists
between the object and the poet's mind. As in the painting of
Dali (and what Dali found in Chirico), the whole world of
horizons and perspectives has been realigned, restudied, re-
thought out, in terms of a true perspective. Again, as in Surrealist
painting, the direct line in a poem or a painting is difficult
to follow.

This world of startling perspectives is not, as in Eliot, for
example, and in many contemporary poets, one of private associations. It is a world, rather, of poetry based on the most impersonal associations. Truth itself appears impersonal, because
it is not given in terms of physical laws which have been breaking down since the discovery of the laws of fourth dimension.
The poet's discovery of the nonphysical nature of the physical
world now derives from his intelligence and directs the imposi-
tion and the collage of his images. The whole question of gravity
and of the operations of gravity which have preoccupied the
Western mind in the twentieth century are evident in Eluard's
poetry, where the laws of gravity are defined in terms of a metaphysical urgency. He recognizes, as do scientists, the incoherency
of a world picture; he is equally concerned, as is any scientist,
about the discovery of a possible coherency, however incoherent
the plasticity of an object might be.

The immediate point of departure for Eluard is feeling, *la
sensation*, the feeling which is his sense of solitude and the exploration of that solitude. This exploration is especially significant in regard to an awareness concerning the actual physical
properties of things, their existence as apart from the poet's
own. One critic has written that Eluard is "struck, to repeat
Hegel's phrase, not by the abstract essence of objects, but by
their concrete reality."[11] The impressions of his poetry are there-

fore tactile; the idea proceeds from this tactility. The images
in the poem "Comme deux gouttes d'eau" (*La Rose publique*),
for example, depend on the poet's sense perceptions. Eluard's
method is to seek out, to discover, a tactile association from
which the reader may deduce a notion of the abstract ideal he
wishes him to find. The poem thus becomes, on the reader's
part, a discovery coexistent with the poet's discovery. Eluard
writes:

> Il [l'homme] imposait sa voix inquiète
> A la chevelure dénouée
> Il cherchait cette chance de cristal
> L'oreille blonde acquise aux vérités.

(He imposed his troubled voice / Upon the unbound hair / He
looked for that chance of crystal / The blond ear acquired by truths.)

The *chevelure dénouée* exists for Eluard. He sees the object
in itself, unlike Baudelaire, where a similar image would not only
exist as a symbol and as a part of a myth, but also as a present
experience; and unlike Mallarmé, where an attempt would be
made to seize the image-object as part of an overall aesthetic
synthesis. The important word in these lines is *cherchait*, where
the quest implied in the sense of the verb is the noun, *cristal*.
The fragility of the accessory object, *oreille*, is not called *cristal*,
but summons up another object which, since it is already in the
possessions of the poet's mind, is *cristal*. The most accurate
description of understanding of an object is in terms of what
has happened to it; in the passage just quoted, *acquise aux
vérités*. Further, this exploration is extended to the most significant of all "other" or alien situations, that of a woman. As is
usual in Eluard's love poetry, man is represented by darkness,
the woman by light: *Il offrait un ciel terne à des regards sensibles
de la vie* "He offered a dark sky to the sensitive glances of life"
("Comme deux gouttes d'eau"). The glances of the woman are
called *levriers sensibles de la vie* ("the sensitive hounds of life").
In line with the impersonal view of objects, these glances are not
like *levriers*; rather they are, to the poet's mind, *levriers* because
they fulfill the same function of speed. Again the man is represented by the opposite of speed, by "his memory which sank

into the sand" (*sa mémoire qui s'ensablait*). Eluard returns to
the image of light, the characteristic of woman; water, again
a female association, music:

> *L'amour unique tendait tous les pièges du prisme*
> *Des sources mêlées à des sources*
> *Un clavier de neige dans la nuit.*

(The single light holds all the traps of the prism / Springs mixed
with springs / A keyboard of snow in the night.)

Underlying these approaches to the objective real is a desire to
change the world.

Again it is a problem of dealing with his inner aloneness;
hopefully, it could be possible to unite his own feelings with a
hidden meaning of the objective world. This desire changes the
objective reality: Eluard would, in finding the hidden meaning
of objects, be able—especially if the occasion be fortuitous—to
amalgamate them to his inner psyche of everchanging, everflow-
ing self. Eluard sees life and the world about him, and therefore
objects, as double; they are capable of being changed because
of their inherent nature:

> *Une nuit de métamorphoses*
> *Avec des plaintes des grimaces*
> *Et des rancunes à se pendre.*

(A night of metamorphoses / With lamentations grimaces / And
ill-feelings to be clung to.)

III   The Appearance of the Object

The role of the poet, as Eluard understands it, and as
Baudelaire also taught, is to be the one who reveals the hidden,
mysterious, psychic life lying—almost in wait—beneath the external world of objective appearance. The role of the poet would
also include that of the painter; and of all the painters of today,
it is perhaps Picasso who shows to us a kind of magical world
or psychical life in the most mundane objects. In Eluard's poem
dedicated to his friend Picasso, the reader may discover how the

poet approaches the object from the viewpoint of the mystery it contains and how the poet illustrates for others the credibility of such mystery. The first part of the poem deals with surprise, the poetic element most basic to a magician. The poem is fairly direct: Eluard recounts the meeting of friends again. As a background to this event, Eluard writes of the sky:

> *J'ai vu le ciel très grand*
> *Le beau regard des gens privés de tout*
> *Plage distante où personne n'aborde.*

(I saw the sky very large / The fine glance of people deprived of everything / A distant beach where no one lands.)

The image of the beach gives the reader an emotional constant for the idea of distance and loneliness. Eluard continues in the first part:

> *Bonne journée qui commença mélancolique*
> *Noire sous les arbres verts*
> *Mais qui soudain trempée d'aurore*
> *M'entra dans le coeur par surprise.*

(Wonderful day which began with melancholy / Black under the green trees / But which suddenly soaked with dawn / Entered into my heart by surprise.)

From the beach to the sky, the image of Eluard's poem proceeds as does his thought.

In the second half of the poem the poet seeks those objects which correlate with the achievement of the painter. Eluard invokes Picasso as a magician, "this man ... who said fingers make the earth rise" (*cet homme ... qui disait les doigts font monter la terre*). The view of reality of what is painted is no more restricted to the actual object of the painting than are the objects in the poem. Eluard tries to find objects which, when acted upon, indicate artistic control, discipline, enchantment, significance, all attributes of painting:

> *L'arc-en-ciel qui se noue le serpent qui roule*
> *Le miroir de chair où perle un enfant*

Et ces mains tranquilles qui vont leur chemin
Nues obéissantes réduisant l'espace
Chargées de désirs et d'images
L'une suivant l'autre aiguilles de la même horloge.

(The rainbow which becomes twisted the serpent which rolls along / The mirror of flesh wherein a child makes pearls / And these tranquil hands which go their way / Obedient clouds reducing spaces / Burdened with desires and images / One following the other hands of the same clock.)

What the poet, as well as the painter, is looking for is the clear vision of the object, not its subjective correlative; he would see it anew and afresh, as a means of understanding. And from this understanding of objects comes an understanding of his solitude. First, however, must come understanding, which, for both poet and painter, means vision. Eluard involves the world so that he may have a precise vision of the objective world:

Montrez-moi le ciel chargé de nuages
Répétant le monde enfoui sous mes paupières
Montrez-moi le ciel dans une seule étoile
Je vois bien la terre sans être ébloui
Les pierres obscures les herbes fantômes
Ces grands verres d'eau ces grands blocs d'ambre des paysages
Les jeux du feu et de la cendre
Les géographies solenelles des limites humaines.

(Show me the sky charted with clouds / Repeating the world hidden under my eyelids / Show me the sky in a single star / I really see the earth without being dazzled / The dark stones the phantom grasses / These great glasses of water these great chunks of amber of the landscapes / The interplay of fire and ash / The solemn geographies of human limits.

Eluard calls upon love and his power and control over love; he becomes a kind of magician of love: *ces filles noires et pures qui sont d'ici de passage et d'ailleurs à mon gré* ("these dark and pure girls who are here temporarily and elsewhere to my liking"). Eluard's greatest wish is to possess the knowledge of secrets, the secrets which unite the images of love with the splendors of the earth:

> *Montrez-moi ces secrets qui unissent leurs temples*
> *A ces palais absents qui font monter la terre.*

(Show me these secrets which unite their temples / To those absent palaces which make the earth rise.)

Eluard's method, all through the quest for an accurate knowledge of the object, is to add to a sensitive, perceptive feeling (*sensibilité*) one of sympathy (*pathétique*). The *sensibilité* is a way of knowledge; the *pathétique* relieves the metaphysical and aesthetic preoccupations from too mechanical and too reflective a tone. The use of such empathy makes possible a further enjoyment of the poetry through an understanding on a direct level. The reader has a somewhat similar feeling in reading Rimbaud, for example, in his verse: *J'écrivais des silences, des nuits, je notais l'inexprimable. Je fixais des vertiges* ("I wrote of *silences, of nights, I noted down the inexpressible. I stabilized dizziness*"). The meaning is difficult to paraphrase; the immediacy of the experience is felt by the reader through an identity of suffering and struggle. Further, the empathy on the reader's part is equal to the freedom (*disponibilité*) of the poet when writing a verse. The readiness of both poet and reader is fixed on the concreteness of the object, through which—again—the beautiful shines forth.

Underlying a concept of the knowledge of an object is the continuity of the poet's own self, despite the fact that all is change. This continuity is one of his own solitude, which is unchanging. From this solitude comes an extensive awareness of all surrounding objects, which he must strive to understand. What does not change is the poet's role to see, each day, each object anew:

> *Nous vivons dans l'oubli de nos métamorphoses*
> *Le jour est paresseux la nuit est active*
> *Un bol d'air à midi filtre et l'use*
> *La nuit ne laisse pas de poussière sur nous.*
> ("Notre mouvement," *Le Dur désir de durer*)

(We live in the forgetting of our metamorphoses / The day is lazy
the night is active / A bowl of air at noon filters the day and wears it
out / The night does not leave any dust upon us.)

The continuance of life, of renewed vision and earned knowledge, is the "echo" Eluard describes as the way he "hears" and
"sees" and understands in *Le Dur désir de durer*. The object
maintains itself; the question is one of the poet maintaining himself in the face of the world as it is. For all aspects of life, in
Eluard, come together to form a many-faceted whole:

> *Mais cet écho qui roule tout le long du jour*
> *Cet écho hors du temps d'angoisse et de caresses*
> *Cet enchaînment brut des mots insipides*
> *Et des mondes sensibles son soleil est double.* (*Ibid.*)

(But this echo which rolls all through the day / This echo outside
of the time of anguish or of caresses / This brutish chaining together
of insipid words / With sensitive worlds its sun is double.)

Eluard would never stand still, secure in the knowledge he
has achieved. As are most writers in the twentieth century, he
is filled with distress (*inquiétude*) stemming from his consciousness of being alone in the world. This aloneness must solve the
dilemma a contemporary poet is faced with: He can be overcome (*vaincu*) by the world and its horrors, ending up with
"the bitter laughter of the man overcome by the world" (*ce
rire amer / De l'homme vaincu*") of Baudelaire's poem "Ob-
sessions." Or else he must try to affirm a way of knowledge of
some sort. To deny reality, the real real, as the Surrealist revolution attempted to do, because that reality precisely leads to
the "bitter laughter," brings a poet to search for a path to a
knowledge of reality whereby it becomes possible to write
poetry, that is, to discover meaning in the world. The world
exists and one must see it, one must undergo the visible experience of a garden, of the absence of another person, of skies, of
the horror of war. Eluard's achievement is all the greater because, starting with premises generally Hegelian in origin—the
search for the Absolute—he never abandons hope. In "Paroles
peintes" (*Cours naturel*), Eluard writes:

Pour réunir aile et rosée
Coeur et nuage jour et nuit
Fenêtres et pays de partout

Pour abolir
La grimace du zéro
Qui demain roulera sur l'or
. . . .
Pour que les déserts soient dans l'ombre
Au lieu d'être dans
Mon
Ombre
Donner
Mon
Bien
Donner
Mon
Droit.

(In order to unite wing and dew / Heart and cloud day and night / Windows and countries from everywhere / In order to abolish / The grimace of the zero / Which tomorrow will roll upon the gold / In order that the desert might be in the shadows / Instead of being in / My / Shadow / To give / My / Good / To give / My / Right.)

Eluard believes himself to be the "slave" of a view of reality which would bring together all that he sees and feels; he strives to bind this reality, through poetry, to his own solitude. In *La Rose publique*, he entitles one poem "L'objectivité poétique n'existe que dans la succession, dans l'enchaînement de tous les éléments subjectifs dont le poète est, jusqu'à nouvel ordre, non le maître, mais l'esclave" ("Poetic objectivity exists only in the succession, in the linking of all the subjective elements of which the poet is, until new orders, not the master, but the slave"). From a theory of knowledge Eluard thus proceeds to a theory of poetry and what poetry should accomplish. The purpose of poetry is more than knowledge; it also implies a means of renewing vision and bringing oneself into the external world and bringing the external world into one's own psyche. The significance of poetry then becomes a further understanding of private anguish (*inquiétude*) and a further understanding of individual aloneness.

CHAPTER 5

Reality of the Word:
the Chemistry of Poetry

I   A Poetics of Things Seen

A key phrase to Eluard's theory of poetry is the title to the
book of poems, A l'intérieur de la vue (*Within the Limits
of Vision*). In "Le Cinquième poème visible" of this collection,
Eluard begins with the words:

> Je vis dans les images innombrables de saisons
> Et des années.

(I live in the innumerable images of the seasons / And the years.)

Eluard finds poetry to be necessarily *visible*, something seen.
The whole problem of a visual art is the principal concern of
poets today. The concept of poetry has slowly but surely evolved
over the past two hundred years towards a doctrine of inner
vision. First of all, for most poets today, poetry should not teach:
It should not be a means of instruction as a replacement for
prose. The eighteenth century in France had thought of poetry
as simply rimed prose. With the Romantic revolution and the
influence and example of Chateaubriand, poetry became something seen; and in seeing, felt. The primary sense was sight: the
picturesque aspects of landscape, the varied beauties of nature.
By the end of the century, with the example and practice of
the late Hugo, Baudelaire and Rimbaud, vision ceased to be
poetic emotion ancillary to what was seen or visually perceived
outside the poet's mind.

Finally, vision became inward; the secret meaning of what
was seen became of primary importance. Eluard's poetic belief

88

affirms the significance of such inner vision. Meaning is not interpreted as philosophical in intent, having meaning by definition. The purpose of poetry becomes an attempt on the part of the inner vision to free the outer vision from any other pre-occupation than a realization of a beauty deriving from the inner vision. Poetry ceases, moreover, to relate an anecdote or a happening. In other words, it ceases to be retrospective; it gains a purpose of magic, of prophecy; the poet becomes the seer. When Eluard writes that he has seen *images innombrables*, in the sense that he lives them, rather than stating a historical fact of a past experience, he states how he lives in the ever-present storehouse of images forming the matter of his poetry. The images can be found everywhere:

> *Je vis dans des images innombrables de la vie*
> *Dans la dentelle*
> *Dans formes des couleurs des gestes des paroles*
> *Dans la beauté surprise.*

(I live in the innumerable images of life / In the lace / Of the shapes the colors the gestures the words / In unexpected beauty.)

Eluard thus uses the exterior world to discover a more profound understanding of experience. Baudelaire, in an article on Marceline Desbordes-Valmore (in *L'Art romantique*), had written: "I have taken pleasure in seeking in outside and visible nature examples and metaphors which would serve me in characterizing the pleasure and impressions of a spiritual order."[1] Baudelaire's use of image indicates the poet's spiritual longing. For Eluard the images thus come upon do not serve as means of characterizing an inner state (turmoil, spiritual anguish, spleen, *idéal*) to the extent that they do in Baudelaire. Instead, the poet, in Eluard's view, projects himself into these images because therein lies the secret of understanding the meaning which is there; and, as usual with Eluard, the self-projection is a means of coming to terms with his own solitude. Eluard, as does Baudelaire, knows that in the exterior *spectacle* the sudden revelation of the intensity of being alive takes place.

Baudelaire had further written (in *Fusées*): "In certain states of the soul which are almost supernatural, the depth of life is

revealed quite completely in the sight (*le spectacle*), however
commonplace it may be, that lies before one's eyes."[2] For Eluard
the spectacle (the storehouse of images) does not become anything, least of all a symbol. Eluard seems to foretell the problem of the *nouveau roman* of Robbe-Grillet, who writes that it
is impossible for nature to participate in our secret sorrows
and anguish: The novelist describes this problem as a tragic
error of a humanist writer (cf. Camus).

For Eluard, as for Baudelaire, the poet's task is to come upon
beauty in images, to vanquish the beauty inherent in them—
a veritable struggle of Jacob with the angel—by making the
beautiful shine through an image. In line with French aesthetics
from the eighteenth century on, Eluard finds beauty in "every-
day ugliness" (*dans la laideur commune*); again Eluard thinks
of "love" or regard for the ugly as an affirmation of the experience of living or seeing which are basically the same. The
reader, in trying to understand Eluard's use of images, thinks
of the late Picasso who could make, literally forge, sculpture
out of bicycle parts and junk ("The Goat"). The line of poets
who make a poem is parallel to the line of painters who make
a painting by using materials the ordinary person would consider unworthy of art. The aesthetic notion implied in this
belief is much deeper than nineteenth-century writings based
on the commonplace as a source of content (Zola) or the
humble life as having a kind of pathetic affective value
(Coppée).

Eluard's great originality, moreover, stems from his intellectual
delight in love which is, itself, a source of the beautiful. In the
poem entitled "Le Cinquième Poème visible" (*A l'Intérieur de
la vue*), he speaks of clarity: *Dans la clarté fraîche aux pensées
chaudes aux désirs* ("In the cool clearness with thoughts warm
with desire"). The key word is *clarté*: the poet inspects all the
possibilities of a given experience in an aspect of light; he thus
understands any object in itself and the beauty of the object
(or situation) in itself. For Eluard an experience of sight has
an eventual life-giving meaning:

> *Je vis dans la misère et la tristesse et je résiste*
> *Je vis malgré la mort. (Ibid.)*

(I live in misery and sorrow and I hold out / I live in spite of death.)

There follow statements, introduced by the words *je vis,* at the beginning of each stanza, which indicate the triple sources of Eluard's poetry. In the first part of this section Eluard writes:

> *Je vis dans la rivière atténuée et flamboyante*
> *Sombre et limpide*
> *Rivière d'yeux et de paupières*
> *Dans la forêt sans air dans la prairie béate*
> *Vers une mer au loin nouée au ciel perdu.*

(I live in the river (which is) diminished and blazing / Dark and limpid / River of eyes and eyelids / In the airless forest in the smug prairie / Towards a sea in the distance bound to the lost sky.)

The reader perceives in these lines the poet's emotional tone and mental state which are revealed in the images. The *rivière* is, obviously, not the river of life which flows: Its flowing nature is its own. The condition of dream and change in the poet's experience is his own. The two are not one, nor is the one symbolized by the other. Eluard follows a theory of poetry of psychological description very close to Laforgue's when the earlier poet writes: "I am thinking of a poetry which would be like psychology but without the dream-form, with flowers, odors, inextricable symphonies with a melodic phrase (a subject), the design of which reaffirms itself from time to time."[3] The deeper significance of the river lies in the melodic or musical effect: In the passage from Eluard just quoted, the repetition of the sound *r* (*rivière, sombre, rivière, paupières, forêt, prairie, vers, mer*), culminating in the verb *perdu,* gives a sense of the river's movement; it also gives a sense of the poet's state of dream. The melodic pattern of the verse, the flowing quality of the river, the dream of the poet, although not used as symbols one for the other, are tied together in a melodic, psychological, poetry. Further, like Laforgue, Eluard does not try to write a meaningful poetry, that is, a poetry which has a direct and paraphrasable content. The so-called expository nature of verse, which could be possible with poetry written in the nineteenth century, is not a true poetry, either for Laforgue or for Eluard. Laforgue writes: "I am thinking of a poetry which would say nothing, one which would consist of bits of disconnected rêverie. When a writer wants to mean, explain, prove something, you have prose."[4] Eluard's poetic conviction is, then, psychological; he clearly takes attitudes and makes judgments. Yet these positions in themselves are not poetic; he does not fuse them onto the image. The reader sees the two qualifications of the *rivière, atténuée et flamboyante, sombre et limpide,* which represent both the quality of the poet's dream-state as well as the dual nature of human experience, even in a moral way of good and evil.

It is possible that, for Eluard, the dream-state is more significant than "psychological" states definable in set terms. The dream is an inner world of perception which has its own melody or form (*dessein*), its own laws or structure. These laws of the inner world differ from melody or form; they also have their own entity apart from the structure of the poem. The poet's originality lies in the capacity to find separate states in a three-part division of psychic life (or experience), dream, and exterior phenomena. Eluard differs from Laforgue in that the desire to show these relationships is less apparent. Eluard is closer to Mallarmé because, for Eluard, the poem simply exists through a power of words which can be experienced and therefore be. Eluard's attempt, moreover, brings in a further problem of inspiration.

The correlative association implied in *ciel perdu* implies a place for inspiration similar to Ovid's in *Ars Amatoria* (Book III): "There is a god within us; we are in touch with heaven: from celestial places comes our inspiration" (*Est deus in nobis et sunt commercia coeli; / Sedibus aetheris spiritus ille venit*). Inspiration is a basic quality of French aesthetics. In the seventeenth century, a protest against inspiration as stemming from instinct against the irrational in man and poet is reflected in Fontenelle's critical disapproval of "poetic rage" and enthusiasm (*fureur et enthousiasme*).[5] These two terms become a part of the Romantic creed; they remained, on the whole, simply a kind of baggage of the Romantic poet. With Baudelaire, Rimbaud and Lautréamont, both poetic notions became learned and willed (*voulu*). With the Surrealist revolution such learning and such power of the will went even deeper and depended upon the deepest instincts of the subconscious; under Freudian influence the Surrealists sought in Freud a *raison d'être* for these subconscious drives.

The greatest paradox of such a drive or impulse based on the deliberate exploration of instinct is that, many times, it takes the form of a search for vaster landscapes. This search is a way of escape from solitude; or rather a way of establishing a distance from that solitude. The distance thus established spatially enables the poet to understand the content and significance of his solitude. Eluard writes "towards the sea in the distance" (*vers une mer au loin*). In Baudelaire the notion of voyage and distance is of first importance. The Surrealists, as did Baudelaire, sought in a willed condition or state a new world of the psyche and the possibility of an infinite world. Eluard, again like Baudelaire, is concerned with "the martyrs of an evil way," *martyrs d'un chemin mauvais* ("L'Irréparable"). A feeling of exile is not so strong in Eluard as in Baudelaire; Eluard tries to find in the "evil way" a more concrete conception of a new era and a better world. The "vast appetite" ("*vaste appétit*") of Baudelaire is, with Eluard, not so much a capacity for exile as it is for understanding. Moreover, the "transfigured universe" (*l'univers transfiguré*) in Baudelaire is a literal remaking of the world. For Eluard, the universe simply becomes itself through the instinctual understanding of the poet. Both protest with equal vehemence against the mediocrity of life. Both speak to their "solitary brother" (*frère solitaire*) as a mediation between themselves and poetry:

> *Je vis dans le désert d'un peuple pétrifié*
> *Dans le fourmillement de l'homme solitaire*
> *Et dans mes frères retrouvés.*
> ("Le Cinquième Poème visible,"
> *A l'Intérieur de la vue*)

(I live in the desert of a petrified people / In the swarming of a solitary man / And in my brothers that I have found again.)

The "transfigured universe," for Eluard, is based on a reading
of the dual aspect of the world; or, rather, in the poetic vision,
the poet sees opposites come together to form a single meta-
morphosed unity:

> *Je vis en même temps dans la famine et l'abondance . .*
> *Dans le désarroi du jour et dans l'ordre des ténèbres. (Ibid.)*

(I live at the same time in famine and abundance / In the disarray
of light and in the order of shadows.)

The doctrine of opposites forms the basis of Eluard's poetics;
it gives his imagery a quality of unexpectedness and yet of
rightness. There is a truth of imagery which, in turn, is founded
on an affirmation of life. In this respect Eluard departs from
Dadaism and the extremes of Surrealism. He halts before the
moment of complete aesthetic principle. In the question of
death—the question of immortality is the most pressing one for
twentieth-century man—Eluard's poetry is an answer:

> *Je réponds de la vie je réponds d'aujourd'hui*
> *Et de demain*
> *Sur la limite et l'étendue*
> *Sur le feu et sur la fumée*
> *Sur la raison sur la folie*
> *Malgré la mort malgré la terre moins réelle*
> *Que les images innombrables de la mort. (Ibid.)*

(I answer for life I answer for today / And for tomorrow / On
limit and extension / On fire and smoke / On reason and madness / In
spite of death in spite of the less real / Than the innumerable images
of death.)

According to Eluard's belief, the images are thus to be read
as signs. Baudelaire had written: ". . . all is hieroglyphic, and we
know that symbols are obscure only in a relative way, that is,
according to the purity, the good-will or the native clairvoy-
ance of souls."[6] These signs are everywhere present; the world
is itself full of mysteries that the poet should find. The poet,
moreover, discovers these mysteries. Because he has the power

to transmit them in a living form to his poetry, he reflects something of the divine.

> *Je suis sur terre et tout est sur terre avec moi*
> *Les étoiles sont dans mes yeux j'enfante les mystères*
> *A la mesure de la terre suffisante.* (*Ibid.*)

(I am on earth and all is on the earth with me / I give birth to mysteries / In tempo with the adequate earth.)

In one important aspect Eluard differs from Baudelaire (and this difference is especially true of the later poetry written during his post-Surrealism period) in that the intention is eventually transfigured into an utilitarianism of human good:

> *La mémoire et l'espoir n'ont pas pour bornes les mystères*
> *Mais de fonder la vie de demain d'aujourd'hui.* (*Ibid.*)

(Memory and hope do not have mysteries for boundaries / But building the life of tomorrow from today.)

In the poem "Sans âge" (*Cours naturel*), the reader further discovers certain poetic beliefs of Eluard. A poet escapes from his solitude by means of his poetry, by means of his capacity to discover images; in discovering images, he defines his own freedom and that of others:

> *Et je ne suis pas seul*
> *Mille images en moi multiplient ma lumière*
> *Mille regards pareils égalisent la chair*
> *C'est l'oiseau c'est l'enfant c'est le roc c'est la plaine*
> *Qui se mêlent à nous.*

(And I am not alone / A thousand images in me multiply my light / A thousand similar glances equalize the flesh / It is the bird it is the child it is the rock it is the plain / Which lose themselves in us.)

In Eluard an awareness of the variety of phenomena outside himself takes the place of the city crowd in Baudelaire: "Multitude, solitude: equal and convertible terms for the active and productive poet. He who does not know how to people his solitude, does not know how to be alone in a crowd."[7] For Eluard poetry is a means of knowledge of how he comes upon the complexity and variety of his solitude:

> Pour tout comprendre
> Même
> L'arbre au regard de proue
> L'astre adoré des lézards et des lianes
> Même le feu même l'aveugle.
>
> ("Paroles peintes," Cours naturel)

(In order to understand everything / Even / The tree with its look of a ship's prow / The star worshipped by lizards and creepers / Even the fire even the blind man.)

In the search for poetic knowledge, the poetic state (état poétique) frequently involves the possible rejection of both memory (souvenir) and the past (expérience). In one way, to be attached to the past makes it impossible to render god-like (diviniser) either ourselves or our present condition.

II Vision and Language

The state of poetic creativity lies in the notion of the way of looking at objects, or rather, the poet's attitude towards language.[8] For Eluard, the making of a poetic image is not the same thing as "poetization." In Les Sentiers et les routes de la poésie, Eluard describes the poetic state:

The poet, waiting, as for any other lesson, for obscure news of the world and the improbable problem of grass, pebbles, dirt, splendors, which is spread out under our steps, will render the delights of the present language as well as that of the man in the street or the wiseman, as well as that of a woman, a child, or a madman. If one wished there would be only wonders.[9]

The poetic state is, therefore, basically one of communication: Speaking out from his own solitude, the poet tries to find a kind of truth to which both he and another can suscribe. But it is a communication founded on poetic vision. The poet himself—through his own will—forms preconceived notions, aesthetic or otherwise. Again, to go back to the idea of the Absolute, the poet, once he has understood that the way of vision is the way of truth, will inevitably find a way of communication to reach others. The difficulty of Eluard's poetry comes from precisely this fact, that the vision is true, but the reader has become used to "poetic" poetry, one which is not true, possessing a false literariness.

In the poem "Règnes" (*Le Livre ouvert* I), the vision is clear, unobscured, even direct, as we have noted before. The reader, however, might find it difficult to "read" the poem until he grasps the sense of the absoluteness of the image which comes forth; he experiences precisely the same effect in reading Racine, though Racine's poetry is more concerned with the psychological absolute or universal:

> *Les fleurs les feuilles les épines*
> *Redevinrent visibles*
> *Les bourgeons et la rosée*
> *Virent le jour*
>
> *Sur le fleuve de mai*
> *La voile écarlate*
> *Fit battre le pouls du vent*
>
> *Sous couleur de vie et d'espace*
> *Sous formes de légers nuages*
> *Sans un frisson*
> *Le sein de l'aube consentait.*

(The flowers the leaves the thorns / Became visible again / The birds and the dew / Saw the day / Upon the river of May / A scarlet sail / Caused the pulse of the wind to beat / Under the color of life and space / Under the form of light clouds / Without a shudder / The breast of dawn gave consent.)

The primary means of communication is that of the "delights of the purest language" (*délices du langage le plus pur*). These delights come from a freedom of the mind, rather than from a kind of concentration the reader expects to find in Valéry. The freedom of the mind (*détente de l'esprit*, in Breton's words), makes possible the discovery of relationships between two seemingly unrelated objects.[10] In the last verse cited above, *le sein de l'aube consentait*, the reader would first think of Valéry and suspect that Eluard has used a similar kind of poetic technique of extreme concentration, of bringing two ends of a series of thoughts together; Valéry then leaves the connection between the thoughts to the intellectual grasp of the reader.

The element of poetic surprise in Valéry, moreover, comes after the intellectual. For Eluard, the question is not one of concentration, of compression. It is rather one of "freedom" (*détente*), wherein the two ends of a train of thought depend upon the extent to which the reader grasps the poet's vision: It is the poet who has seized the necessary relationship (*rapport*). Poetic surprise occurs because the relationship is absolute. The intention of both Valéry and Eluard is an eventual clarity, an inevitable awareness of a denuded idea of the self and the world, of individual aloneness, and a kind of alienation from the world. The clarity of Eluard's poetry, however, derives from the surprise of the discovery of relationships between objects. The effect on poetry is to make it less opaque,[11] and to make his own solitude more bearable.

The eventual result of such release from opaqueness is the liberation of the individual. The liberation of the individual is a fundamental use of the will (*volonté*) for the Surrealists; from the desire and the will for an individual personal freedom come a similar will and desire for the freedom of the language. Eluard would free language from any kind of stricture imposed by an *a priori* concept of its usefulness or its relationship to other words. He once wrote that he would free poetry from being "... the more or less learned, the more or less happy, assemblage of vowels, consonants, syllables, words."[12] Eluard carries Mallarmé's poetic doctrine to its ultimate conclusion; starting from Mallarmé's idea of "giving a new meaning to the words of the tribe" (*donner aux mots de la tribu un sens nouveau*), Eluard moves the liberation of words according to their inherent freedom that cannot be imposed by the poet.

Eluard believes as strongly as did Verlaine in the necessary musical quality of verse; yet this musical quality must again be free. It must be born from the necessary, although unexpected, discovery of words in relationship to or in conjunction with other words. Eluard refuses the Romantic notion of musicality that sought an orchestrated effect typical of nineteenth-century Romantic poetry that corresponded to tone poems in music. Again Eluard protested against such musicality. The attempt, especially on the part of the Parnassians, to write "literature," as though literature existed apart from the freedom of man and from the inherent belief in the absoluteness of that freedom, aroused Eluard to write that poetry is the contrary of literature and that poetry "happily maintains the ambiguity between the language of truth and the language of creation" (*entretient heureusement l'équivoque entre le langage de la vérité et le langage de la création*). The truth of a poetic statement tries to reach over and come to terms with the situation as it exists. When the statement and the situation balance, poetry can be said to have come about. For example, in "Rencontres" (*Le Livre ouvert* I), a similar ambiguity (*équivoque*) is evident in the following lines:

> *Jeune arbre idole mince et nue*
> *Unique source caresse haute.*

(Young tree thin and nude idol / Only source high caress.)

Where the tree exists, in itself, *jeune, mince, unique,* the truth of the existence of the tree is *idole, source, caresse;* that truth is the poet's understanding of the existence of the tree.

Criticism of the "literary" value of poetry implies a more profound philosophy of creation, or rather, of the purpose of creation insofar as the poet and the making of poetry are concerned. For the Surrealists go back to Baudelaire and to his docrtine of *correspondances,* in the discovery, in the unveiling, in the coming upon by surprise of the hidden tension between the "language of truth" (*le langage de la vérité*) and the "language of creation" (*le langage de la création*); the truth or the absolute relationship between the two becomes clear. The danger is the risk the poet takes that he might not be able to carry out, in the writing of the poem, what he has deciphered.[13] The use of *correspondances,* therefore, depends much more on the breaking of the willful or contrived awareness of the poet in his search for *correspondances* than is true in Baudelaire. In one way, Eluard is much less the maker of poems, a *faber,* than is Baudelaire, and certainly Mallarmé. Eluard discovers in the relationship between the two sorts of language, that which is "above" (*en haut*) and that which is "below" (*en bas*), not a world of illusion, but one of truth:

> *Ténèbres abyssales toutes tendues vers une*
> *confusion éblouissante, je ne m'aperçois pas*
> *que ton nom devenait illusoire, qu'il n'était*
> *plus sur ma bouche et que, peu à peu, le*
> *visage des tentations apparaissait réel,*
> *entier seul. C'est alors que je me retournais*
> *vers toi.* ("Nuits partagées," *La Vie immédiate*)

(Unfathomable shadows all sketched out towards a dazzling confusion, I do not perceive that your name became illusory, that it was no longer on my mouth and that, little by little, the face of temptations appeared more real, entire, alone. It was then that I turned around towards you.)

The discovery of the meaning of *correspondances* lies in the freedom of the image itself; the use of *correspondances* as a kind of intellectual or critical analogy would not give the movement in depth that the poetic understanding would require.[14]

The reason for the movement in depth is the persistent preoccupation with time, with the limits that time imposes upon the individual poet, especially in terms of his individual aloneness, his persistent solitude. Eluard is not faced with the threat of time before the poetic work is achieved (as is Keats); the French poet is more concerned with the constant going away and returning of moments of perception, the understanding of *correspondances,* and the moments in which he actually lives the contemporary event. In Eliot, for example, there are also two senses of time: the moment of insight, the "moment in the garden"; and the moment of history, of current events.[15] Eluard sets himself in revolt against time in either sense. He destroys time insofar as the succession of time is concerned. As one critic has written about Eluard's poetry: "all is simultaneous, all is eternal" (*Tout est simultané, instantané, éternel*).[16] The poet does not construct the poem either as existing in space (as does Baudelaire in "Le Balcon," for example); nor does he devise a counterpoint of time which allows a freedom to have both kinds of "Eliotian" time (as does Proust). Eluard faces an anguish of time as honestly as does Pascal; Eluard cannot go back to a prestructured religious belief of an absolute, but must—necessarily—find it for himself as the poem is being written.

Nor is it true that Eluard might conceive a realization of a "continued awareness of time" (*durée*) in any one other solution: Eliot's religion, Pascal's continued anguish, Baudelaire's Romantic poetization, or Proust's technical achievement. For Eluard must seek another solution, one that allows him to flee from any mechanical or mechanistic view of time. Eluard's solution is to see the world as purely as possible, almost as eternally present; his view of the world implies that the present moment contains a dimension of continual return and is therefore eternal:

> *Sur un pré blanc des nuages blancs*
> *Descendant corriger la terre*
> *L'azur est à peine plus fort*
> *Tous les regards vont s'éclaircir*
> *Délivrer la nature blanche.* ("Rencontre," *Le Livre ouvert* I)

(On a white meadow white clouds / Come down and correct the earth / The blue sky is scarcely more strong / All glances become more and more clear / Deliver white nature.)

The effect is one of time in timelessness through a use of the infinitives *corriger* and *délivrer;* the repeated use of the adjective *blanc* denotes a kind of universality.

III   *Poetic Invention*

The escape from time, or the mechanical constancy of time, is a part of poetic invention. The poet invents, in the etymologi-

cal meaning of coming upon, the necessary relationship between
the "language of truth" and the "language of creation." Within
such invention all the metamorphoses of truth (*vérité*) into
creation (*création*) and creation (*création*) into truth (*vérité*)
become possible, again according to the absoluteness of poetic
vision:

> *La droite laisse couler le sable*
> *Toutes les transformations sont possibles.*
> *Loin, le soleil aiguise sur les pierres sa hâte d'en finir.*
> *La description du paysage importe peu,*
> *Tout juste l'agréable durée des moissons.*
> *Clair avec mes yeux,*
> *Comme l'eau et le feu.* ("L'Invention," *Répétitions*)

(The right side lets the sand run / All transformations are possible /
Afar, the sun sharpens his never-ending haste on the rocks / The
description of the landscape matters little, / Just the pleasant dura-
tions of the harvests. / Clear with my eyes, / Like the water and
the fire.)

Between the writing of the poem and the emotional situation
which has called it forth, there is, as Breton termed it, a point
where the two must come together, a "living source" (*foyer
vivant*). The difficulty for the reader is to share with the poet,
to coexperience with the poet, the moments where the writing
of the poem and the emotional situation come together.

In the passage just quoted, the emotional situation could
be the view of a sunset over a field, a commonplace of poetry;
the emotional situation must search out and discover, invent,
the poetic means. The poetic means are not descriptive; they
are rather the use of words which, taken together in their
inevitable rightness, fuse the emotion of a situation to a poem, in
this case the lines, *Clair avec mes yeux,* / *Comme l'eau et le
feu.* Even here the use of the word *comme* is not used in its
allegorical sense; the implication is that the clearness of water
and fire are perceived with the poet's eye, not that the eye
sees a "continued awareness" (*durée*) of the harvests (*moissons*)
as a kind of fire or water because of the pureness of these two
elements.

Again Eluard tries to make a poem grow organically and avoids a literary tendency towards making allegories or comparisons, where each part of the allegory remains apart because each part exists in its own right and not because it has grown and sent down roots into the poet's subconscious. Each poem thus becomes an example of the vital force or affirmation of a drive (*élan*) which endows the poem with a power that it would not otherwise have. (*I. e.*, the sunset would remain a picture of a sunset.) In another way, the poem is an affirmation of the poetic self (*soi*), seeking liberty from the words it must both admire and disdain. It is the duality of attitude which gives the words of a poem both a meaning of their own and a power of suggestion, as in the following lines from "Après moi le sommeil" (*Cours naturel*):

> *Plusieurs douceurs entrevues*
> *Toutes plus mignonnes*
> *Que le cri de la fleur amie*
> *Avaient fondu dans la nuit*
> *Comme clefs dans leurs serrures*
> *Comme boisson dans la chaleur.*

(Several tendernesses glimpsed / All sweeter / Than the cry of the friendly flower / Had melted in the night / Like keys in their locks / Like drink in the heat.)

Further, the seeking of an ultimate reason in the self not only for being, but also for any act, is close to Romanticism. The Surrealist experiments gave greater range to the sway of the self and to the defense of the individual's right to find in himself the rules of poetry and writing verse. In the lines just quoted, the verse *avaient fondu dans la nuit* is given meaning by the last two verses of the stanza: *Comme clefs dans leurs serrures / Comme boisson dans la chaleur.* These two lines depend for their significance upon the poet's own belief in the justness and the appropriateness of his own individual visual experience. The poetic state thus established is close to Platonic inspiration; this state also illustrates poetic fury, which very often is the condition of the poet according to Surrealist practice. Eluard, however, never makes such fury be an end in itself nor the only state in which he can operate poetically. His poetry skims close to the communicable ideal and does not sink into obscurities of private automatic associations.

Eluard derives from Baudelaire in that both poets seek some sort of "mystic nourishment" (*mystique aliment*, "L'Ennemi") as an escape from contradictory forces within themselves and also as a means of discovering strength (*vigueur*). Eluard writes:

> *Par ta force et par ta faiblesse, tu croyais*
> *pouvoir concilier les désaccords de la présence*
> *et les harmonies de l'absence, une union*
> *maladroit, naïve, et la science des*
> *privations. Mais, plus bas que tout, il y*
> *avait l'ennui. Que veux-tu que cet aigle aux*
> *yeux crevés retienne de nos nostalgies?*
>
> ("Nuits partagées," *La Vie immédiate*)

(By your strength and by your weakness, you thought you were able to reconcile the disharmonies of presence and the harmonies of absence, a clumsy union, simple, and knowledge of privations. But, deeper than anything else, there was boredom. What do you expect that this eagle with blinded eyes should keep of our nostalgias?)

For many poets the source of a force within themselves is a hidden life, even a life beforehand as with Rimbaud. Rimbaud is far more spiritual, far more a *mystique à l'état sauvage*, than Eluard could ever be. The reader does not find in Eluard's poetry a notion that the poet would want another life which would draw him away from and separate him from the life he is living at the moment. That life was often filled with every kind of sadness, distress, war, hatred, meanness Eluard acknowledged and fought against. Yet the life that he showed he lived was not a life apart. The theory of poetry that he upheld was basically that of an individual who seeks to see and to understand so that he might live the life of a poet.

In *Donner à voir* he had written: "I became a slave of the pure faculty of seeing, slave of my unreal and virgin eyes, ignorant of the world and of themselves. Quiet power. I suppressed the visible and the invisible" (*Je devins esclave de la faculté pure de voir, esclave de mes yeux irréels et vierges, ignorants du monde et d'eux-mêmes. Puissance tranquille. Je supprimai le visible et l'invisible*). A basic hold of life and a kind of poetic fury against all injustice led Eluard to write a political poetry; the force of love for another person became a love for all mankind. The two are inevitably linked in Eluard:

> *Mains par nos mains reconnues*
> *Lèvres à nos lèvres confondues*
> *Les premières chaleurs florales*
> *Alliées à la fraîcheur du sang*
> *Le prisme respire avec nous*
> *Aube abondante....* ("Sans âge," *Cours naturel*) [17]

(Hands recognized by our hands / Lips merged with our lips / The first floral warmth / United with the coolness of the blood / The prism breathes with us / Abundant dawn.)

The hands reaching out to other hands became more and more the preoccupations of Eluard's poetry; the meaning of his individual solitude gained in significance as the themes of his poetry became more and more central to these preoccupations. His concern over political solutions to social problems broadened, deepening the current of interests which flows through all that he had written. It is another aspect of depth in his poetry.

CHAPTER 6

Reality and Vision: the Human Condition

I Moral Intent and Social Function in Poetry

ONE of the most significant questions in twentieth-century literature is that of bringing together literature and a belief in social betterment. A significant attempt to do so has been *Unanimisme*, dating back to 1906.[1] The principles of this movement (as reflected, for example, in Jules Romains' *L'Ame des hommes* of 1904 and *La Vie unanime* of 1908) are ones basic to the problem of literature and the poet's involvement in social problems. They include: the value and importance of a group working together in a kind of collective movement; group psychology; eventually, a sort of social mysticism. *Unanimisme* also imposed certain criteria for poetry. The mission of the poet is to bring all people together, wherever they are, into a feeling of solidarity and group accomplishment. While there is little direct influence of *Unanimisme* on Eluard, his verse does reflect the affirmative part of *Unanimisme* in that the poet, according to Eluard, should be concerned with what goes on outside or around him. Eluard's concern also shows a certain influence of Rousseau: The poet asserts that the world has been created good and beautiful, with possibilities of human understanding; he further asserts that men have prevented themselves from mutual understanding by their own prejudices and misunderstandings. All of Eluard's poetry possesses an underlying optimism; he seems to comfort himself that a poet, even through poetry, is able to find again a lost Eden or Paradise. The metamorphoses on the poetic or aesthetic level should also be efficacious on the social level. Moreover, a kind of idealism that seeks the Absolute is also clearly reflected in Eluard's idealism: He believed that men, through a feeling of fraternity, could make such idealism possible. Eluard was no fatalist: He did not accept

106

an inevitability in either the consequences or the direction of history. He always made a very firm and very virile stand against all that would make man less than he was, or less than he had the possibility of being. Eluard's poetry is, on the whole, one of hope.

The title of a collection of poems, *Poésie ininterrompue*,[2] gives the clue to the significance of his concern. *Ininterrompue* means that the poet's life is a continuous one of seeing, an uninterrupted act of understanding, a life moreover of "love" and of participation, whether pleasant or difficult, that strives always towards a notion of happiness, despite the continued anguish of solitude. For Eluard, to seize and to identify his own happiness in participation with others was his "reason for being a poet." This participation also gave meaning to the lives of others. And for Eluard such a transmission of meaning was an imperious necessity: Poetry is uninterrupted. The title of the collection implies that the individual is the basis for a socially better future. The title poem bears a quotation from Tristan Tzara's *L'Antitête*: "Resistance is organized on all pure foreheads" (*La résistance s'organise sur tous les fronts purs.*) "Poésie ininterrompue," the title poem, is a poem of purity. It is a call to purity to all those who would falsify life, who would make life less pure. It illustrates Eluard's moral idealism. The qualities of his vision are a widening of his view of the world and a gaining or an acquiring of density in his poetry. Poems based on this vision become endowed with a fullness, almost spiritual in nature, which has to do with friendship and fraternity, with self-abnegation towards the rights of others. Poetry thus becomes a path towards light: The image of light is the guide by which a poet struggles for, and eventually attains, a completeness of vision which gives strength and vigor to other qualities of his understanding: beauty, love, absolute idea, aesthetic enjoyment in the play of images and words. Further, the dedication of the poem reads: "I dedicate these pages to those who will misread them and who will not like them" (*Je dédie ces pages à ceux qui les liront mal et à ceux qui ne les aimeront pas.*) Eluard's moral courage forces him to speak out against those who do not fight for human liberty; against those who limit the possibilities of fraternal searching for a better life and for happiness; against those who would willfully remain blind to the need to see human needs clearly.

The first part of the poem lists the characteristics of woman. Eluard seeks to describe the duality of his own self by describing the eternal fascination and mystery of woman, all that he is not, all that he has the capacity to be. For Eluard cannot separate the experience of love from the experience of his knowledge of mankind, as an answer to his own definition of his aloneness. He describes all the varied roles of woman, such as have been discussed in the chapter on the love poetry:

> *Nue effacée ensommeillée*
> *Choisie sublime solitaire*
> *Profonde oblique matinale*
>
> . . . .
>
> *Inaltérable contractée*
> *Parée construite vitrifiée*
> *Globale haute populaire*
> *Barrée gardée contradictoire.*

(Nude unobtrusive drowsy / Chosen sublime lonely / Deep oblique early rising / . . . Unvarying contracted / Adorned constructed vitrified / Global high popular / Barred guarded contradictory.)

The search for identity—himself in relation to others—starts with a most profound notion of awareness he can conceive: the presence and absence of the woman he loves. Eluard asks himself: "Are we two or am I alone" (*Sommes-nous deux ou suis-je solitaire*). His poet's solitude is reinforced by his apartness from the woman he loves, and therefore his apartness from others, an apartness which he must overcome. He sees the mystery of life just as his poetry is a mysterious deciphering (*déchiffrement*) of objects about him and of his search for being:

> *Comme une femme solitaire*
> *Qui dessine pour parler*
> *Dans le désert*
> *Et pour voir devant elle.*

(Like a woman alone / Who draws in order to speak / In the desert / And in order to see in front of her.)

Eluard reviews the past:

> *L'année pourrait être heureuse*
> *Un été en barres*
> *Et l'hiver la neige est un lit bien fait*
> *Quant au printemps on s'en détache*
> *Avec des ailes bien formées.*

(The year could have been happy / A summer of iron-bars / And in winter the snow is a well-made bed / As for spring one breaks loose from it / With well-formed wings.)

The reader finds in these lines an element of flight, or of poetic fancy, in the sense that Eluard's thought carries him away from himself in order that he might come back closer to himself. Eluard can never escape, in the final analysis of himself and of the world, from himself in terms of his own solitude, or from others, who also live—inescapably—in terms of their solitude. Thus Eluard always remains a part of the world; he always wishes to maintain a sense of being with others and of being a part of their lives through a mutual sense of anguish:

> *Rien ne peut déranger l'ordre de la lumière*
> *Où je ne suis que moi-même*
> *Et ce que j'aime*
> *Et sur la table*
> *Ce pot plein d'eau et le pain du repas*
> *Au fil des mains drapées d'eau claire*
> *Au fil de pain pour la main friande.*

(Nothing can upset the order of light / Wherein I am only myself / And that which I love / And on the table / This pot full of water and the daily bread / Even with hands draped with clear water / Even with bread made for the eager hand.)

Existence thus comes to mean, for Eluard, not an escape from life in a sort of self-centered pseudomystical "opening out" (*épanouissement*). Eluard cannot imagine a life alone; he experiences a necessity of communication which must be realized so that, in turn, he can communicate with others. He is also fulfilled at the same time that he fulfills the life of someone else: The phrase "the hope of living here" (*l'espoir de vivre ici*) indicates the dual aspect of his love, both for the woman in-

volved and for mankind. Eluard's final poems further indicate a
continually increasing desire to bring about, both in himself
and in his poetry, events which could either bring hope or
despair. In so doing he believes that he takes on a total understanding of the loves and the experiences that others have gone
through; he also sees his own life in terms of its aloneness and
its apartness far more objectively than otherwise would be
the case:

> *Aujourd'hui l'enfance entière*
> *Changeant la vie en lumière*
> *Sans passé sans lendemain*
> *Aujourd'hui rêve de nuit*
> *Au grand jour, tout se délivre*
> *Aujourd'hui je suis toujours.*

(Today complete childhood / Changing life into light / Without
a past without a tomorrow / Today night's dream / In the bright
light all is delivered / Today I am always.)

Aragon says that what is most "obsessing in Eluard's poetry is
the attempt to make it fix with words a certain privileged vision
offered from time to time to the poet."[3] For Eluard this privileged moment includes not only moments of love, but also a
glimpse of the absolute. It receives it most fixed and permanent
form in the understanding of what it means to the poet to communicate to others a perception of love and an evocation of the
absolute. Eluards wants his vision to be shared by others; in
sharing it with others the vision becomes fuller and, in a sense,
more true because it includes the most varied range possible. In
thus reconstituting the present moment so that it becomes an
eternal moment, a *moment de toujours*, the poet and the woman
he loves, the momentary and fragmentary image of sky and
flower, man's need for fraternal understanding—taken together
—lose none of their power to remake the individual concerned
into a person more capable of understanding; and in understanding, the individual avoids the dismay and the loss involved
in a purely time situation:

> *L'homme en butte au passé*
> *Et qui toujours regrette*

> *Isolé quotidien*
> *Dénué responsable.*

(Man exposed to his past / And who always regrets / Isolated each day / Denuded responsible.)

In these lines there is apparent the French tradition of the moralists, of those who comment and seek to define the precise nature of the human condition. For Eluard the lesson to be derived from a view of the lasting moment and enduring time is the assurance that each of such moments has value and is worthwhile, not only because of the way men escape from time, but also because each individual becomes—in a way—a part of someone else and of others. It is a lesson, in Eluard's words, of *la vie immédiate*, of immediacy. Moreover, for Eluard, life considered from this point of view involves a kind of affection or tenderness towards, and a confidence in, his fellowmen:

> *L'on m'aimera car j'aime par-dessus tout ordre*
> *Et suis prêt à tout pour l'avenir de tous*
> *Et je ne connais rien à l'avenir*
> *Mais j'aime et je mourrai d'amour.*

(I will be loved because I love, above all, order / And am ready for everything for the future of everyone / And I know nothing of the future / But I love and I shall die of love.)

In loving others, Eluard feels himself to be "re-invented," or re-defined. His own suffering finds a parallel in the sufferings of others and of mankind in general. From his awareness of suffering Eluard derives an energy which constantly reinforces his poetic vision:

> *Et tous les vivants nous ressemblent*
> *Tous les vivants que nous aimons*
> *Les autres sont imaginaires*
> *Faux et cernés de leur néant*
> *Mais il nous faut lutter contre eux*
> *Ils vivent à coups de poignard*
> *Ils parlent comme un meuble de plaisir*
> *A l'écho des cloches de plomb*
> *A la mutité d'un or noir.*

(And all those living resemble us / All those living whom we love / The others are imaginary / False and closed in upon by their nothingness / But we must fight against them / They live by dagger thrusts / They speak as a piece of furniture creaks / Their lips tremble with pleasure / At the echo of lead bells / At the dumbness of a black gold.)

Again the reader perceives in these lines Eluard's moral intention. Aragon defines such intentions as the "*giving* us to this image of man, marvelously happy, simplified, penetrating, penetrated . . ."[4] Once more the question becomes one of a kind of ineffable poetry; the problem is then how to put what is unutterable in words into words and how to find expression for any absence that the poet might feel:

> *A chanter des plages humaines*
> *Pour toi la vivante que j'aime*
> *Et pour tous ceux que nous aimons*
> *Qui n'ont envie que de s'aimer*
> *Je finirai bien par barrer la route*
> *Au flot des rêves imposés*
> *Je finirai par me retrouver*
> *Nous prendrons possession du monde.*

(To sing of the human beaches / For you the living woman whom I love / And for all those whom we love / Whose only desire is to love / I shall truly end up by barring the way / To the stream of dreams which have been imposed / I shall truly end up by finding myself again / We shall take possession of the world.)

II *Towards a Poetry of Persuasion*

Eluard's vision of the world is unique; as Pierre Emmanuel has remarked, it is one "which only man could have and which is henceforth possible only through this man."[5] Eluard's achievement is that he has been able to bring together an individual vision and a vision which is valid for everyone. Poetry becomes a way of action. Eluard, later in his career, wrote poetry which could possibly be called an apology for a stated political credo; yet in "La Poésie ininterrompue" Eluard still proposes the fundamental problem of the twentieth century. It is impossible for an individual to maintain a point of view based on reason when the individual is faced with the fact of being pushed by some mysterious force so that—once freed from conventions and a stale rhetoric—he must necessarily become involved in action. Such a necessity further propelled Eluard: The implicit idea in his view that all men must come together in understanding had to end in a common action and involvement (*engagement*). The dilemma of poetry which is politically meaningful is that it ceases to be poetry and becomes a means towards an end which it does not define.

Eluard's thought derives, ultimately, from the irrationalism of Surrealism. On the level of speculation, Eluard does not seek to find philosophical categories or mathematical axioms. Eluard does not seek to rationalize his intuitions. Rather, in the words of Emmanuel, "he digs out his intuitions inside his sensibility."[6] Eluard's sensibility is essentially humanitarian; his concern remains with another person involved, even with definitions of personalities taken in time as they evolve through history. He defines personality always in its context with the personalities of those who are in a similar dilemma of understanding themselves and trying to reach out and communicate with one another as they seek to overcome individual feelings of solitude. The notion of politics as a kind of *mystique* certainly tempted Eluard. Quite probably he saw that any statement involving people has to touch upon the way people work. In the twentieth century this means of operation would be a political one: the religious one being—for Eluard and for many intellectuals—no longer viable. Moreover, Eluard was probably mistaken in thinking he could find in Marxism a doctrine of action. It is true that Marxism depends on a dynamic and historical sense and that it has replaced many irrational positions at the beginning of the century. The mistake comes, usually, when Marxism is taken as a kind of rational position towards understanding and controlling history and, therefore, the direction of men's lives toward good. Basically, it remains on a level of substitute mysticism. Again in "La Poésie ininterrompue," Eluard succeeds most when he restricts his sensibility to that point where he is most original: the discovery and exploration of images, always beginning his understanding with a statement of all that sets him aside from others and a suggestion of how to deal with this apartness:

Je n'ai plus de regrets
Plus noir plus lourd est mon passé
Plus léger et limpide est l'enfant que j'étais
L'enfant que je serai
Et la femme que je protège
La femme dont j'assume
L'éternelle confiance.

(I have no regrets / Darker heavier is my past / Lighter is the child I was / The child I will be / And the woman I protect / The woman whose eternal confidence I take on.)

The problem Eluard faces in identifying with others, especially with a woman, is that, once again, he is involved with the self, the *moi*. And it is the self that acts and tries to find answers to the inevitable absurdity of the world. Eluard, moreover, seeks an escape from history in a world in which a religious answer is no longer possible. The poem thus tends to read as a taking account; this accounting explains the long list of experiences in the lines quoted above: the weight of the past, the attitude towards woman, the question of communication, seeing signs and deciphering them, the eternal fascination with woman. Such an inventory is saved from the danger of being simply an inventory by placing it in a timeless situation, by viewing it in terms of universality. Again, as Emmanuel has remarked, "... even in his desperate negation, the poet's experience, however distinctive it may appear, is at the same time, universal in that it is not a feeling of resentment which summarizes it, but a taking account."[7] Eluard sees all things as though they were done for the first time: Each act—however common such an action may be—assumes a position in timelessness; it becomes more than an act, it becomes close to myth and to the eternal symbols of each act:

Et la première différence
Entre des êtres fraternels
Et la première ressemblance
Entre des êtres différents

Le premier champ de neige vierge
Pour un enfant né en été

> *Le premier lait entre les lèvres*
> *D'un fils de chair de sang secret.*

(And the first difference / Between fraternal beings / And the first resemblance / Between different beings / The first field of virgin snow / For a child born in summer / The first milk between the lips / Of a son of a secret blood.)

Here Eluard attempts to explore all aspects of the human condition, refusing to accept in itself any given model or preconceived notion of an act. For Eluard there is "another way of humanity possible": the fullest possible exploration of the resources of the mind to discover and maintain a happiness that is not a synonym for an unawareness, but one that is founded upon an awareness of others and of the concrete experiences for good that are possible. For Eluard, it is a part of a poet's task to fulfill an awareness for others towards others. In this way his own existence becomes existent, his own solitude is made meaningful:

> *D'une rue*
> *D'une rue ma défiguration*
> *Au profit de tous et de toutes*
> *Les inconnues dans la poussière*
> *Ma solitude mon absence.*

(Of a street / Of a street my defiguration / For the profit of all men and of all women / The unknown women in the dust / My solitude my absence.)

Eluard here reaches the furthest extent, or the furthest purity, of the fundamental tenets implicit in unanimism. The earlier experience grew out of concerns which had to do with history and the historical and political moment as well as with concerns for literature. Eluard's concern for the betterment of others grows out of a very strong conviction for the love of others; he wishes to be faithful in his relationship with the woman he loves. Again, added to Eluard's idea of the universal, is a concept of faithfulness and of an individual being faithful. Thus the individual self is engaged, wholeheartedly and without regret, in an understanding of men.

Eluard in this way forms his images simultaneously; all actions tend to take place as though seen in one glance. The movement of a poem does not come from a back-and-forth view of an object and then of himself. The focus of the eye remains constant on the object; nor does Eluard tend to limit such movement. On the contrary, it becomes more and more vast; it sweeps and extends itself. This vastness makes the reader think of Claudel's *poésie cosmique*:

> La loi feuille morte et la voile tombée
> La loi la lampe éteinte et le plaisir gâché
> La nourriture sacrifiée l'amour absurde
> La neige sale et l'aile inerte et la vieillesse
> Sur les champs au ciel étroit
> Soc du néant sur les tombes.

(The law dead leaf and the fallen veil / The law the extinguished lamp and spoilt pleasure / Food sacrificed absurd love / Dirty snow the inert wing and old age / Upon the fields with a narrow sky / Ploughshare of the void upon the tombs.)

Moreover, in such poetry where intent is directed towards a preoccupation with the ideal, poetry many times becomes rhetorical and loses in poetical intensity. Eluard, in writing such poetry, confronts a necessity to avoid a rhetorical attitude; at the same time, he wants to be able to maintain a possibility of convincing the reader. He must never lose control over the image: Its symbolic nature should never dominate over its presence as an image and as a source of poetic pleasure:

> Ils méditent leur absence
> Et se cachent dans leur ombre.
> Ils ont été au présent
> Ceci entre parenthèses.

(They meditate upon their absence / And hide themselves in their shadows / They have been in the present / This between parentheses.)

The relationship between poetic intent and poetic pleasure is difficult to ascertain in view of a poet's sincerity. If the poet is sincere and believes in the cause he is espousing, then the pleasure the individual reader should receive must be commensurate with the intensity of a poet's feeling. In the case of Victor Hugo, for example, criticism could be directed against his philosophical views; yet Péguy (in *Victor Marie, comte Hugo*) praised the artistic success of *Booz endormi;* Claudel, who detested Hugo's unorthodox religious ideas, wrote that, compared to the French seventeenth-century writers, Hugo's verse is "infinitely more full of color, richer, more sonorous than [French] classical verse, he speaks more to our senses."[8] In Eluard's case, the later verse retains the vigor of the earlier. Yet the reader wonders to what extent the vigor is due to political, and not poetic, intent.

The vigor is due to an idea found in the content; the ideas forming the content spring from a collective conscience dependent on a single political credo. Durkheim's statement that "social facts can be reduced to a force superior to the spirit of the individual" does not allow for the very basis of poetry, that the spirit of the individual is at the very root of a truly poetic experience. In one way it is a return to Herder's romantic notion of the collective soul. Jules Romain had spoken of the "constraint of collectivity" (*contrainte de la collectivité*). The moral grandeur or force of a poem should, however, reside in a poet's struggle, rather than in the dignity of a collective conscience. Much of Eluard's later poetry retains a certain *grandeur;* yet it reads frequently rather as a statement of political purpose than as intimate personal verse. Eluard became more and more attached to a larger vision from *Les Yeux fertiles,* then *Donner à voir* and *Médieuses.* He made an effort to take part in the lives of others; this effort is a perfectly legitimate attitude for a poet if an increase in poetic vision does occur, as for example, in these lines:

> Je vois brûler l'eau pure du matin
> Je vais de fleur en fleur sur un corps auroral
> Midi qui dort je veux l'entourer de clameurs
> L'honorer dans son jour de senteurs de lueurs.

(I see the pure water burning and the grass of the morning / I go from flower to flower upon an auroral body / Noon which sleeps

I want to surround with shouts / Honor it in its day of perfumes
and glimmerings of light.)

Eluard attempts to join a collective vision with a personal
vision:

> *C'est très vite*
> *La liberté conquise*
> *La liberté feuille de mai*
> *Chauffée à blanc.*

(It is very quick / Liberty conquered / Liberty leaf of May /
Brought to a white heat.)

Further, the kind of mystique evolved around human solidarity
and human help is a noble one. Yet how a poet can relate such
a mystique to an individual poetic act of having seen (*avoir vu*)
some image, of having formed some concept of others from the
vantage point of his own private anguish is difficult to understand. It is possible to try and seize some sort of mystique or
rhythm of the world (*rhythme du monde qui travaille et qui
souffre*), and then make room for it in poetry:

> *Et le feu aux nuages*
> *Et le feu dans les caves*
> *Et les hommes dehors*
> *Et les hommes partout*
> *Tenant toute la place*
> *Abattant les murailles.*

(And the fire with clouds / And the fires in the cellars / And men
outside / Men everywhere / Holding the entire public square /
Breaking down the walls.)

Poetry has power because it affirms the world as the poet sees
it. Poetry as an affirmation can be moving and can be a viable
poetic statement:

> *[les hommes]*
> *Se partageant le pain*
> *Dévêtant le soleil*
> *S'embrassant sur le front*

> *Habillant les orages*
> *Et s'embrassant les mains*
> *Faisant fleurir charnel*
> *Et le temps et l'espace.*

([men] sharing each other's bread / Unrobing the sun / Hugging each other to their foreheads / Clothing the storms / Holding each other by their hands / Causing both time and space to flower bodily.)

The reality of the world exists; it must be seized, even in all of its aspects. By enlarging his notion of the love of a woman to include love of mankind, Eluard gives breadth and depth to his poetic vision. As he has tried to understand the image, the object, the idea of love in all of its duality, so he tries to understand the world of men in the same spirit of hope and poetry. For the eventual meaning, not of the poem but of a poetic existence, is to give to men a complete world, a totality of vision which leads to freedom and hope. Poetic tone is thus enriched; lyricism breaks away from a purely private manner to a larger field of belief.

In his "Chant du dernier délai" (*Poèmes politiques* [Political Poems]), Eluard describes the usefulness of poetry; he describes it in a larger context of belief in human values which have the power to overcome the poet's solitude. He begins by indicating the darkness of his life and of all that surrounds him. This darkness comes from the dark night of the soul due not to the absence of God, but to an absence of a relationship with others. In that relationship Eluard finds himself completed and fulfilled, while—at the same time—he finds himself as an individual; his poetic solitude is fulfilled in a similar manner:

> *Noir c'est mon nom quand je m'éveille*
> . . . .
> *Noir où la flèche s'est plantée*
> *Où le tison a prospéré*
> *Noir le gentil corps foudroyé*
> *Noir le coeur pur de mon amour*
> *Noire la rage aux cheveux blancs*
> *A la bouche basse et baveuse.*

(Black is my name when I awake / . . . . Black where the arrow has planted itself / Where the half-burned wood has prospered /

Black the noble body struck down / Black the pure heart of my love /
Black the madness with the white hair / With the mouth low and
slobbery.)

The mystical experience continues. Eluard wonders when his
anguish will end: *Cette envie folle de hurler / Ne cessera
qu'avec ma voix* ("This mad desire to scream / Will end only
with my voice"). He goes back to his beginnings and finds
there a notion of being born again as a part of the lives of
others: *J'étais construit les mains ensemble* ("I was made hand
in hand"). This awareness of others gives him a sense of solidarity and firmness and direction. Now, in a moment of darkness, he discovers himself lost, torn away from that solidarity:
*Mais aujourd'hui je me sens mes os / Se fendre sous le froid
parfait* ("But today I feel my bones / Break under the perfect
cold"). His aloneness takes on all aspects of religious anguish:
apartness from the world (*Je sens le monde disparaître*, "I feel
the world disappearing"); nothingness, a void, a *néant* (*Rien
ne demeure de nos rires / Ni de nos nuits ni de nos rêves*,
"Nothing remains of our laughter / Nor of our dreams"); a
spiritual acedia, where complete exhaustion prevents any further
experience of the kind of communion he requires (*J'ai trop
pleuré la coque est vide / Où nous ne pouvions qu'être deux*,
"I have wept too much the shell is empty / Wherein we were
able to be but two").

Since Baudelaire, the modern reader of poetry has been
accustomed to read poetry for no other reason than the poem
itself. If he succeeds in finding a philosophy or a principle of
moral action in studying the poem, such interest lies, theoreti-
cally, beyond the existence of a poem as a poem. The success
of a poem lies within the limits imposed by use of image and
levels of ambiguity. In the Renaissance, however, the purpose
of poetry was, frequently, to inspire men to better actions; its
intent was moral. In understanding the moral intent of Eluard's
later verse, we must remember the caution given by T. S. Eliot:

... we must avoid being seduced into one or the other of two extreme opinions. The first is, that it is simply the value of the *ideas*
expressed in a poem which gives the value of the poetry; or that it
is the *truth* of his view of life—by which we ordinarily mean its
congruity with our own—that matters.[9]

Eliot goes on to show that poets, Lucretius and Dante, took philosophies already in current intellectual usage and sought then "to convey an emotional equivalent for the ideas." In Eluard's political poetry, it is precisely the emotional search for a better life, for a more honest approach to the solution of human problems, that gives his later poetry value. In reading a stanza, for example, such as the following,

> *Ecartez-vous de ma douleur*
> *Elle vient droit de la poussière*
> *Elle nie tous les sacrifices*
> *Le mort n'est jamais vertueuse*
> *Ecartez-vous de vivre sans mourir.*
> ("Chant du dernier délai," *Poèmes politiques*)

(Stand away from my pain / It comes straight from the dust / It denies all sacrifices / Death is never virtuous / Stand away from living without dying.)

the rhetoric of persuasion comes close to destroying the value of the poem as an equivalent, or a search for an equivalent, of the anger, distress, dismay the poet experiences, to the reader through images and through the general tone of the poem. The reader is moved not by the rhetoric which calls upon his intellect for a response and for an affirmation of belief, but by the poet's anguish and sincerity. The success of the poem derives from the emotion based on, in Eliot's phrase, "what it feels like to hold certain beliefs." The reader is concerned with, interested in, the poet's emotional tone; or rather, the reader looks for a success a poet has in arousing in the reader an emotion similar to, if not identical with, his own. The purpose of poetry for the modern reader is just such an attitude towards the use of poetry. And for Eliot a distinction is to be made between the social obligation of a poet as a member of society and his "social" obligation as a poet, which is to preserve the language of his country. In Eluard's later verse, many times the poet's language arouses empathy in the reader not towards the poet's feelings, but—on the contrary—towards the ideas or the ideational content of the poetry. Eluard is most successful when he is the least close to a stated political credo

and when he speaks again from a universal point of view; he is
closer to his reader when his poetry becomes more "cosmic" and
less particularized within the limits imposed by a particular
political allegiance:

> Laissez-moi donc juger de ce qui m'aide à vivre
> Mon désir de fraîcheur a consumé les fièvres
> Neige sous le soleil je suis né d'une femme
> Parfois j'ai sa vertu
> Le golfe de son ventre fait les hommes libres.
>   (Ibid.)

(Let me then be the judge of that which helps me live / My
desire for coolness has consumed the fevers / Snow under the sun
I was born of a woman / Sometimes I have her virtue / The gulf
of her womb has made men free.)

At other times, in "La Poésie doit avoir pour but la vérité pra-
tique," (Poèmes politiques), the tone and texture of the poetry
tend to become rhetorical; the reader does not participate in
terms of emotion in the poet's experience; the poet's external
concerns tend more to take the place of a viable emotional
experience:

> Mais si je chante sans détours ma rue entière
> Et mon pays entier comme une rue sans fin
> Vous ne me croyez plus vous allez au désert
> Car vous marchez sans but sans savoir que les hommes
> Ont besoin d'être unis d'espérer de lutter
> Pour expliquer le monde et pour le transformer.

(But if I sing plainly my entire street / And my entire country
like an endless street / You no longer believe me you go to the
desert / Because you walk aimlessly without knowing that men /
Need to be united for hoping for struggling / For explaining the
world and transforming it.)

Here the intent of the aesthetic preoccupation, which has been
with "explaining the world" (explication du monde) as an
emotional experience and with "transforming the world" (transformation du monde) from a viewpoint of poetic vision, leans

towards intellectual persuasion; such persuasion, in view of the intent of imagery, is not primarily the intent of poetry. In Eluard's earlier verse, the reader's interest is maintained not only because of the poet's sincerity, but also because of the affective value of the poem, as in tragedy. Again, as in tragedy, when the interest is removed from the affective to the intellectual or conceptual, the poem, as a poem in what it is trying to do, loses in force and even power and beauty. In reading Eluard, one is constantly moved by the presence of solitude: To what purpose and for what reason this solitude should be used is of secondary interest. The primary interest is that the reader should be moved and should participate in the poem which is a true creation of that aloneness.

CHAPTER 7

Metamorphoses of Reality:
The Poet and the Tradition

I Eluard and the Nature of Tradition

IN a study of Eluard, after an understanding of his age and a reading of his poetry, the reader asks himself where Eluard stands in relation to a tradition of poetry. A poet must use the tradition in which he writes: The tradition imposes not only means, but also problems which have to be solved. These are problems of belief in the need for poetry, of the nature of poetic immediacy, and of understanding on the part of the reader. The reader further asks himself in what way a poet has contributed to the continuance of, or to the breaking away from, that tradition. It is not so much a question of influences. The scholarly investigation of sources and influences is difficult where those influences have been assimilated through the age itself. The sources are not certain, again, where the adaptation to sources is not specific, but only general to the age. In Eluard's case the description of sources and influences, in a precise way, is not as important as is a comparison of how various poets perceived the tradition; a comparison is also necessary between the way these poets modified tradition and the way Eluard continued the modifications. As a poet of his age, when poetry was much discussed, when poets such as Baudelaire, Rimbaud, and Mallarmé were being discovered and commented upon, it is significant to note to what degree Eluard lived in the center of such commentary and evaluation. His poetry shows, directly or indirectly, an appreciation of the tradition in that he was constantly aware of a necessity to evaluate the importance of that tradition; he thought this true of any poet writing in the twentieth century.

Further, other than poets who stand directly in the line of

124

a native tradition or who are being assimilated to that tradition, there is a validity in seeking out comparisons with problems posed by other poets who have faced similiar problems of poetic assimilation of the past. The reader, confronted by the seeming newness and almost disconcerting novelty of Eluard's poetry, tries to judge in this way Eluard's significance and to evaluate Eluard's contribution to the tradition.

The tradition in France which is closest to Eluard is that of the immediate past, the nineteenth century. From Romantic lyricism two developments were derived: the one, that of art for art's sake of Gautier and the later Parnassians; the second, that of an evolution, from Romanticism, towards considerations of social usefulness and general moral purpose. Eluard's position avoids both extremes and attempts to form a middle ground of poetic principle which, in many ways, is similar to Baudelaire's. Eluard's idea of poetry is one that shuns, in the best of his poetry, both extremes, extremes which are evident in the evolution of Surrealist practice from Surrealism as an end in itself to Surrealism in the service of the Revolution. The purest Surrealist poetry of Eluard is a poetry which aims at a perfection of form, within the possible limits of exploration and invention of poetic language. It aims at an understanding of life through the secret power of words. The poet becomes a visionary, standing in his own solitude, as well as a maker of verse.

Eluard thus follows the line of poetry which tends to create myths. The myth of the poet as a creator is the one which most attracted the Surrealists. For Rimbaud the poet is a seer, a *voyant*:

The poet becomes a *seer* by a long, immense, and thought-out disordered state of all the senses (*dérèglement de tous les sens*). All forms of love, suffering, madness, he looks for himself, he exhausts within himself all poisons in order to keep only the quintessences. Ineffable torture wherein he needs all faith, all superhuman strength, wherein he becomes above all others the sick one, the criminal one, the accursed one—and the supremely learned one!—For he arrives at the unknowable. . . . Thus the poet is truly the thief of fire.[1]

Each of Eluard's poems is, in a way, a statement of this mythic role of the poet. Each poem is an exploration of what the

poet has seized of a divine intuition and brought back to earth
with him: the mysterious duality of woman, the image in itself
and in its power to retain life, the external word and the
external world which together make up a form of knowledge
behind which lie the secrets of beauty and meaning, the life
of the inner conscience, the future of man as a fulfillment of
poetry. At times Eluard carries out all of these roles and
becomes truly Orpheus:

> Je change d'idée
> Tu ris tu joues tu es vivante
> Et curieuse un désert se peuplerait pour toi
> Et j'ai confiance
> Fini
> Je n'ai jamais pu t'oublier
> Nous ne nous quitterons jamais
> Il faut donner à la sécurité
> La neige paysanne la meule à ruines
> Une mort convenable
> Le jour en pure perte noie les étoiles
> A la pointe d'un seul regard
> De la même contemplation
> Il faut brûler le sphinx qui nous ressemble
> Et ses yeux de saison
> Et ses mousses de solitude.

("Les Semblables," *La Vie immédiate*)

(I change my idea / You laugh you play you are alive / And
curious a desert would become populated for you / And I am con-
fident / Finished / I have never been able to forget you / We shall
never part / One must give to security / The peasant snow / The
millstone in ruins / A suitable death / The day in pure loss drowns
in the stars / At the point of a single glance / Of the same contemplation / One must burn the sphinx which looks like us / And
its seasonable eyes / And its mosses of solitude.)

The woman in the poem has the capacity to bring about
the contrary of a definition: The desert becomes inhabited.
This experience is the constant amazement of man's encounter
with and meeting with woman. The image of the snow and
the millstone each carries within itself the contrary of its own

nature: The snow is associated with what is most usually thought of as close to earth (*paysanne*); the millstone—which is solid and part of a structure—is ruined. The eternal myth of two qualities, almost anima and animus, constitute a constant tension and pull of the world in which both poet and reader live. All outward aspects of life—death, day, the look of another person—seem to be only appearances behind which the poet comes to an understanding of his own life. His inner conscience is contemplation, the quiet reflection and observation coming from the poet's eye. And his other self, the other person near him, is the unknowable person who must, in a sense, be destroyed and remade; the poet's solitude and aloneness, his existence in measurable time (*saison*), must also be destroyed. Above all, the other person must be brought into communion with the poet's own suffering and aloneness.

Eluard's poetry thus bears witness to a continued redefinition of the Orphic myth. As with Rimbaud, Eluard has experienced all forms of love—suffering, separation, delight—and even hallucination, in order to be able to define himself as a poet and therefore as a man. The poem is a search for the ineffable which lies behind the world of appearances. The poems are each so carefully constructed that they have the power to enable the reader's mind to explore further myth; the reader then becomes —insofar as he is capable—a "thief of fire" (*voleur de feu*). In the exploration of myth, the reader, as well as the poet, comes to glimpse, even for a moment, the arcana of the mysteries.

The exploration of myth goes back to the effort, among certain nineteenth-century poets, to explore the world of the beyond. This attempt is reflected in Hugo's idea of the poet's role as a "sonorous echo" (*écho sonore*): The world is not seen by human eyes, not heard by human ears, but is known only through the incantatory power of a poet's voice. Poetry, in the latter half of the century, tended to become hermetic, occult; the poet becomes a priest, the poem itself becomes a chance— a "throw of the dice" (*coup de dés*) in Mallarmé's phrase— wherein the charm might or might not work, depending on the poet as a priest. Frequently critics apply the word magic and magician to such roles.

Both terms can certainly be applied to Eluard, especially

in view of the solitude in which he works. He seems to stand
alone, and the poem appears an incantation, a carefully worded
prayer, one could almost say. This incantation reaches the
reader's deepest feelings; the poem, moreover, reaches in its
most precise detail a kind of universality of appeal because
it does reconstruct the myths that are a part of each individual's
subconscious. Eluard's poetry frequently has a quality and a
tone similar in appeal to the ineffable and the mystical. His
vocabulary repeats that of the mystics: The unique and the
one are pure terms applied to non-Christian situation. The
element of vision is present in his poetry in an almost cataclysmic
sense: Poetic vision allows him to look into the future:

> *Justice harmonieuse. La rive nord du monde*
> *dissolvait. Les dernières lames de glace*
> *flottantes avaient déjà un cachet d'ancienneté.*
> *Sous un ciel amélioré, des semences d'or vif*
> *chevauchaient paternellement les vestiges de*
> *la vie.*
>   *La mort défalquée, je tranchais la*
> *surface et la masse, l'étendue et la durée;*
> *j'épousais les reliefs imperceptibles de la*
> *fièvre et du délire, sur tous les chemins*
> *au petit bonheur de jours et de nuits sans*
> *violence.*
>
>   ("Le 6e poème visible, iv,"
>   *A l'Intérieure de la vue*)

(Harmonious justice. The north bank of the river dissolved. The
last flowing sheets of ice already had an air of oldness. Under an
old sky, seeds of bright gold straddled paternally the vestiges of life.
    Death abated, I crossed the surface and the mass, extension and
duration; I married the imperceptible reliefs of fever and delirium,
on all the roads towards the quiet happiness of days and nights
without violence.)

In these lines, the reader experiences the poet's solitude;
that is, the poet's vision occurs, as does St. Anthony's temptation
and St. Jerome's learning, in the desert. Eluard, similar to the
modern painter, seeks to be alone so that he may be prepared
for the coming of the vision, that he may be ready to seize upon

the gift of inner sight. Once he has, in a very real way, remade the world, the modern poet (or painter) can then describe it in terms which work on two levels. The first level is spiritual, as in the Christian position where death is overcome, *la mort défalquée*. The second level is physical in all senses of depth and extension of time and space, so that he may live in the world, as does a saint; and like a saint, the poet is not a part of the world since the world is imperfect, deformed, not a true picture either of physical depth or spiritual regeneration arising from creative energy. Again, the poetic experience parallels the way of Christian mysticism in the embracing of fever (*fièvre*) and delirium (*délire*), in order that an ultimate kind of peace—a peace that passes all understanding—be achieved. It is significant that the lines just quoted are from *A l'Intérieur de la vue*. Eluard speaks, as does a mystic or a prophet, from inside the vision; the prophetic role of the poet puts Eluard in the tradition going from Hugo through Rimbaud to Claudel. Eluard is far more refined, far less *sauvage* than is Rimbaud; yet the prophetic visionary voice is present.

The deepest expression of religious feeling is solitude. Here Eluard is close to the Christian tradition of *beata solitudo*. His poetry is a continual redefinition of the loneliness of the modern artist and of modern man. Even in moments of deepest affiliation with another or with others, Eluard still perceives himself as apart and alone. Further, the tone of solitude is one where Eluard speaks most profoundly. One is reminded of Baudelaire's *pensée* (in *Mon coeur mis à nu*): *sentiment de destinée éternellement solitaire* ("feeling of destiny eternally alone"). For Eluard the problem of solitude is most keenly felt in the presence of the woman he loves. He sees her aloneness and finds his own to be parallel to it:

> *Comme une femme solitaire*
> *Force d'être l'une ou l'autre*
> *Et tous les éléments*
> *Je saurai dessiner comme mes mains épousent*
> *La forme de mon corps*
> *Je saurai dessiner comme le jour pénètre*
> *Au fin fond de mes yeux.*
>
> ("Poésie ininterrompue")

(Like a woman alone / By dint of being one or the other / And all the elements / I shall be able to trace as my hands marry / The form of my body / I shall be able to trace as the light of day penetrates / To the very depth of my eyes.)

In Eluard's aloneness, even in his experience of being with another, one thinks of Scève and the very precise and very clear view of love which derives from such an aloneness. The poet discovers himself and the world. All that is nonessential to the experience is stripped away; the total commitment is seen in a clear, pure, light. The effort to view experience in this way finds an aesthetic equivalent in the poet's attitude towards the poem which he wishes to make equally clear, equally precise in its outlines (*dessiné*).

The basic consideration in Eluard's mind is lucidity. The lucidity of love, or rather the expression of love through lucidity, is the lucidity of art. Although Eluard would possibly never equate an art of love with an art of poetry, and although he is quite apart from the courtly tradition of courtly love, still the continuous and continued desire to see love clearly and to write the poem clearly is certainly true. The struggle towards clarity in both a love situation and in a poetic situation go together. The poem reaches its moment of greatest clarity when the presence of love is most clearly experienced:

> La source coulante et douce et nue
> La nuit partout épanouie
> La nuit où nous nous unissons
> Dans une lutte faible et folle
>   X
>   X   X
> Et la nuit qui nous fait injure
> La nuit où se creuse le lit
> Vide de la solitude
> L'avenir d'une agonie.

("Les Sept poèmes d'amour en guerre, iii,"
Au Rendez-vous allemand)

(The fountain running and sweet and nude / Night everywhere opened out / The night wherein we become united / In a weak and mad struggle / And the night which curses us / The night wherein is hollowed out the empty / Bed of solitude / The future of a death agony.)

The tendency in Eluard, as is true of English poetry since Eliot, is to unify all experience into one total experience which may be termed poetic. For Eluard the means of welding and amalgamating the terrifying variety of what happens to a single individual is intellectual: By intellectual, Eluard means that a notion of eternity beyond the present imperfect state of knowledge is a constant presence in the poet's mind. His thinking is Platonic and is more and more in evidence since *La Rose publique*. He also has hope in something better; not that this hope blinds him or causes him to abandon the present and to fall into the heresy of Manichaeism. Rather his idealism makes the present clear, makes him accept the present, makes him want to be a part of the present because it has the potential of something better. Just as each word has the power of a greater good beyond itself and yet remains itself, so each experience—while accepted and not rejected—contains the form of a greater future, a future where the poet will see more clearly the beauty possible in the world he now inhabits.

II   *Eluard and the Intellectual Ideal*

One of the poems of *La Rose publique* has the long title: "Une personnalité toujours nouvelle, toujours différente, l'amour aux sexes confondus dans leur contradiction, surgit sans cesse de la perfection de mes désirs. Toute idée de possession lui est forcément étrangère" ("A personality always new, always different, love, wherein the sexes are confused in their contradiction, arises ceaselessly from the perfection of my desires. All idea of possession is perforce stranger to it.") Eluard intensifies the physical statement by the underlying directive force of his intelligence as it has been shaped and ordered by his awareness of his own solitude. This critical force enables him to give a purity of intellectual ideal (*idée*) to his desires. His need is not for possession, which would be a kind of imperfect joining or welding of the experience of the other person to himself. Eluard seeks to join any experience to an ideal perfection. The

way to such an ideal is through the bringing together, under
the species of intellectual idea, of all experience:

> *J'embrasse avec ferveur la chair des arbres sous leur écorce*
> *Je cherche dans la terre les flammes de la pluie*
> *Les agates de la chaleur*
> *Les plus petites graines du soleil d'hiver.*
> ("Une personnalité toujours nouvelle," *La Rose publique*)

(I embrace with fervor the flesh of trees under their bark / I
seek in the earth the flames of rain / The agates of heat / The smallest
grains of winter sun.)

The key word here is fervor (*ferveur*); *ferveur*, for Eluard,
represents a victory over fatality. Eluard struggles with, and
vanquishes, a fatality which, in the plays of Racine and in
certain novels of Gide, appears to dominate the human predica-
ment. For Eluard, *ferveur* is a necessary part or attribute of
pain (*douleur*). *Douleur* is a significant word in Eluard's
vocabulary. He must, in the midst of a century which compels
each person to face *douleur*, especially in moments of solitude,
discover for himself the manner of overcoming that *douleur*.
In one way, Eluard is in the line of the great French moralists,
from Montaigne on, who teach us lessons of facing *la condition
humaine*. For Eluard the principal lesson to learn is not to
defy pain, or flee from it, or try to make ourselves believe it to
be something else. Eluard shows us that through poetry, through
the kind of idealism his poetic images present, we are given
means of overcoming *douleur*, realizing all the while that pain
is a part of our lives. Eluard's lesson is not to be overcome by
douleur, but to understand; and in understanding it, to love it
for the possibility of good it might bring about.

The traditional understanding of *douleur* has been religious;
the profoundly religious person believes that, with time, the
meaning of pain will be resolved in a greater scheme of things.
For the modern artist the stretch of time towards the future
as an alleviation for *douleur* has not been sufficient to give
meaning to it. Eluard rather feels a necessity of understanding
pain by separating himself from it, by being alone and establishing a distance between it and himself, while he seeks out

images which will make it possible for him to understand it. A failure to understand *douleur* by traditional religious means constitutes, in effect, a kind of deicide; it also leads, at times, towards the dandy (*dandysme*) or towards the noisy, rowdy, aspects of Surrealism (cultism); or even towards "black humor" (*humour noire*). More profoundly, Eluard stands in the tradition of the nonbeliever who has abandoned God, while remaining essentially a religious person. Eluard, as a poet, thinks and creates in religious terms. He writes in "Comme une image" (*L'Amour la poésie* [*Love (and) Poetry*]):

> Muet malheur de l'homme
> Son visage petit matin
> S'ouvre comme une prison
> Ses yeux sont des têtes coupées
> Ses doigts lui servent à compter
> A mesurer à prendre à convaincre
> Ses doigts savent le ligoter.

(Mute misfortune of man / His face dawn / Opens like a prison / His eyes are cut-off heads / His fingers serve him to count / To measure out to take to convince / His fingers know how to bind him.)

From the description of the human condition as a world without God, Eluard affirms life as a force that rebuilds the past and gives meaning to the present; he writes, not in orthodox religious terms, but in terms of a vision of a resurrection on a purely "earthly" level:

> Je sors des caves de l'angoisse
> Des courbes lentes de la peur
> Je tombe dans un puits de plumes
> Pavots je vous retrouve
> Sans y songer
> Dans un miroir fermé
> Vous êtes aussi beaux que des fruits
> Et si lourds ô mes maîtres
> Qu'il vous faut des ailes pour vivre
> O mes rêves.

("Comme une image," *L'Amour la poésie*)

(I come out from the cellars of anguish / Slow curves of ear / I
fail in a well of feathers / Field poppies I find you once more /
Without thinking of it / I am a closed mirror / You are as beautiful
as fruits / And so heavy o my masters / That you need wings to
live / O my dreams.

Eluard's revolt may have mythic connections for twentieth-
century man; spiritually he is seeking the absolute, an absolute
Surreal, which is beyond an intellectual concept of God; God
appears to him a pure state of being which man, as man, frequently does not realize and cannot achieve.

The search for an absolute Surreal frequently, even in Eluard,
gives rise to a feeling of the void of life; he feels that, as a
poet, he confronts the flux of existence. In this flux it is impossible to discover a stable, fixed, movement or pattern either in
the universe or in himself. The feeling of the void makes him
long for death—as in Nerval or Baudelaire or Rimbaud. The
Surrealists were preoccupied with death, and especially with
suicide, as the one supreme Surrealist gesture. The void of life
experienced as the fullness of death is approached as a Surrealist experiment which, by its very concept of experiment,
expresses the most profound notion of stability. Such is certainly the case in Eluard's poetry. The experiment of verse is
a way of achieving stability; the artist seeks the absolute in
death; the Surrealist poet first thinks (and here Mallarmé is
the ancestor) of the death of poetry as the true absolute perfection of the poem.

Further, in place of a traditional religious attitude, Eluard
recognizes the symbolic character of religion: he thus returns
to Heraclitus.[2] And as with Heraclitus, it is language which
points out this symbolic nature. Eluard probably does not find
a resolution of all disparity of viewpoints (social, ethical, even
aesthetic) in an absolute harmony; the absolute of the Surrealists and of Eluard does not indicate such a harmony; nor
does Eluard find an immanent spirit from which springs all
nature or harmony. The three constituent elements of Heraclitus'
view—unity, eternal change, world order underlying all change
—are part of the Surrealist search for an absolute condition
explaining both men's actions and—especially—the significance
of poetry. Language pointed the way to the absolute, and in

being method, became the absolute itself. Language ceased to be symbol (and Eluard's language is not metaphysical), to become the mythic act of the relationship between an immanent principle and a given moment of time and space. The poet is aware of change and of the endless flowing river of time. In "Durer" (*Les Yeux fertiles*) Eluard writes:

> *Une rafale une seule*
> *D'horizon à horizon*
> *Et ainsi sur toute la terre*
> *Pour balayer la poussière*
> *Les myriades de feuilles mortes*
> *Pour dépouiller tous les arbres . . .*

(A gust of wind a single one / From horizon to horizon / And thus on all the earth / To sweep up the dust / Myriads of dead leaves / To strip all the trees.)

The poem continues to show the construction of the world through change. Eluard still looks for an absolute where the self will survive despite the destruction of the world in which it has participated:

> *Fuyante masse faiblesse*
> *Monde qui ne pèse rien*
> *Monde ancien qui m'ignore*
> *Ombre affolée*
> *Je ne serai plus libre que dans d'autres bras.*

(Fleeing mass weakness / World which weighs nothing / Old world which is not aware of me / Maddened shadow / I shall not be more free except in other arms.)

Twentieth-century man, and in this Eluard is typical, sees the passage of time all about him. Proust attempts to overcome it through art, through a nonsegmented time, *durée*. Eluard is concerned more with change in itself, with metamorphosis, with transfiguration. The figura of his poetry—woman, clocks, light— are carried across into the poem according to a secret lesson of their innate oneness, change, in which the shared characteris-

tics unite them. His poetry, which on the surface appears il-
logical, has the logic of being modified outside the "normal"
concepts of time, the fragmented time, which is the time we
have to deal with. Eluard describes the problem, especially
evident from Baudelaire on, of how to make a timeless poetry
from a poetry of time, of making a poetry that communicates
from a poetry that is essentially private anguish.

The problem is essentially one inherent in Novalis (whom
the Surrealists read), who illustrates the dilemma existing between belief in the power of the creative imagination and the
condition of the world as one of the operation of chance, which
comes from God.[3] Surrealism is the furthest extension of idealism from Descartes on. To be, for the Surrealists, is to have
invented a world of one's own; in this world chance should still
exist and the absurdity of the world should exist for the poet,
so that he might know that some logos of Heraclitean harmony
still operates. This harmony underlies a belief in an absolute beauty. Eluard endows poetry with the possibility that
"neither chance nor Providence" has the ultimate say. Poetry,
the creative imagination, creates a true world out of the world
of appearances. Eluard reinvents the world; he does not reject
it; he shows the reader that poetic imagination rearranges the
images and objects of the world in their true relationship. The
import of the world is not the obvious one of imprisonment in
time or alienation from others. The lesson Eluard learned from
a reading of Novalis is that the creative imagination, in moments
of awareness of one's essential aloneness, makes the true psychic
imago; as is Novalis, Eluard is convinced that the *imago* of the
mind that reflects objects or events is the real one. He attempts
to discover means of freeing the image, while—at the same time
—he does not lost conscious direction of the poem. In this
Eluard differs from a pure Surrealism of automation.

Basically, Eluard searches for unity, the unity that gives
meaning to his solitude. However, as Emmanuel has pointed
out, "No one can be reunited to himself, unless it be by a
mediator."[4] An Orphic poet searches for the *médiatrice, both
amante* and *mère,* as do Nerval and Novalis. Eluard's search
ends in a somewhat different manner. Again as Emmanuel has
pointed out: "... Paul Eluard crosses the night, but he will

bring back his Eurydice up to these confines of shadow and
light, of the interior universe and of the world, which are the
true kingdom of poetry."[5] There is a descent into the night in
Eluard; Eluard uses the expression of the mystics. At times he
speaks out like St. John of the Cross and brings back from that
night a sure knowledge of some mediating force between himself and the world. For St. John, it is the living God; for Eluard,
it is a living principle of poetry. For Eluard it is, moreover,
the light of the creative principle which endows his poetry with
meaning and power.

For Eluard, the mediating force is that of love. Oddly enough,
the poet who comes to mind in this respect is Whitman. As Van
Doren has indicated: "... the thing that binds individuals together [for Whitman] is love. Whitman is a great poet because love is necessary to his understanding of the universe, as
it must be for any one who tries to see into the heart of creation."[6] Eluard tries to find in love a force that binds men to
one another. Again Eluard's view is similar to Whitman's thinking in that Eluard believes that love, in all the various aspects
of its reality, is the force that gives a unifying, absolute—if
you will—meaning to the world. The pitch of this love is maintained and gives his poetry a continuity which the variety and
dexterity of his technique only make clearer. Love is very
close to death in both Whitman and Eluard. Van Doren further
remarks: "Heavenly death—it is a commonplace on Whitman's
lips, and he means it literally. For it is through death that he
sees, as he believes, into the heart of creation—where of course
life also is, as sister and bride. At the center of the universe
love and death lie down together."[7]

Eluard further shows ideas of vitalism and life-force current
in the first part of the century. Bergson, for example, believed
it to be possible for one to see into the heart of creation. This
is true of Eluard. His poetry is a constant attempt to find such
a heart. He does not find there a religious reason, but rather a
vital force which maintains the permanence of the world.
Eluard believes, moreover, in a purpose for this search; the
poet's function, in Eluard, is frequently Promethean: A poet
strives and searches in solitude, but achieves a functioning situation towards others. This situation is close to Hugo's ideal

"... to communicate to those below models of superior beauty, to interchange emanations, to carry the central fire to the planet, to put into harmony the various worlds of a system. . . ."[8] Underlying Hugo's statement is an additional sentiment of the Orphic nature of poetry and the poet's role. Eluard also thinks of the poet as Orpheus and accepts a myth of descent and return. He thought it his duty to bear the "sacred fire" (*feu sacré*), to *see* from the anguish of his solitude the ideal world of his meditation. Here again he is close to Hugo when the older poet writes:

The domain of poetry is unlimited. Beneath the real world, there exists an ideal world, which shows itself resplendent to the eyes of those whom serious meditations have accustomed to see in things more than things. The finest works of poetry, of every kind, have revealed this truth, scarcely suspected before, that poetry is not in the form of the ideas, but in the ideas themselves. Poetry is all that is intimate in everything.[9]

The stream of idealism was continued by Mallarmé; Eluard does not see the form, in a descriptive sense, but rather sees before him what is the basic (*intime*) nature of each object. Eluard carries such idealism one step further by showing not comparisons, but this basic quality (*intimité*) between objects and by the Surrealist discovery of how startling such *intimité* can be because the reader has never seen it before as it really is; like Baudelaire, he astonishes the reader by the truth of such *intimité*.

CHAPTER 8

Conclusion

IT is in this truth that the newness of the poet, as proclaimed by Apollinaire (in "L'Esprit nouveau et les poètes" and "La Jolie rousse") must reside. The joining of prophecy to pathos is the especial achièvement of Eluard's poetry. He suffers the present world and, simultaneously, shows the path towards the future. The future is always founded on a coming to terms with his unique solitude and on understanding how, by means of his private anguish, he can reach out to others. For Eluard, such understanding is fundamentally intuitive. Eluard's poetry is a further deepening of the Romantic notion contained in Shelley's phrase: "Poetry is not like reasoning, a power to be exerted according to the determination of the will. A man cannot say, 'I will compose.' The greatest poet even cannot say it."[1] The effort of the will on Eluard's part is rather a determined one to be aware of solitude and from this awareness arises an imaginative power to stir and move the reader.

Notes and References

Chapter One

1. For biographical details, see *Eluard, livre d'identité*, ed. Valette; see also the chronology of Eluard's life to be found in the Pléiade edition, Vol. I.
2. Cf. Louis Perche, *Paul Eluard* (Paris, 1963), p. 89.
3. Paul Eluard, *Poèmes* (Paris, 1951), p. 240. All references to poems quoted will be from this edition, unless separate editions are used. All poems will also be found in the Pléiade edition.
4. Cf. the statement by Tristan Tzara, written much later, in 1950: "Dada was born from a moral demand, from an implacable will to reach a moral absolute, from a deep feeling for man, in the center of all the creations of the mind; it affirmed its pre-eminence over the impoverished notions of human substance, over things dead and possessions indecently acquired. It meant that we wanted to look at the world with new eyes, that we wanted to reconsider at a very basic level, and to feel the rightness of ideas imposed on us by our elders." Quoted in Perche, *op. cit.*, pp. 14–15.
5. For definitions and aims of the Surrealist movement, I have followed Anna Balakian: *Surrealism: The Road to the Absolute* (New York, 1959), pp. 91–164; Wallace Fowlie: *The Age of Surrealism* (Denver and New York, 1950), pp. 105–9; Perche, *op. cit.*, pp. 16–17. The Surrealist documents are found in Maurice Nadeau, *Histoire du surréalisme* (Paris, 1964).
6. Nadeau, *op. cit.*, p. 455.

Chapter Two

1. See Michel Carrouges, *Eluard et Claudel* (Paris, 1945).
2. Paul Eluard, *Capitale de la douleur* (Paris [1924] 1926), p. 137.
3. Paul Valéry, *OEuvres*, I (Paris, 1957), 1338.
4. *Ibid.*, p. 119.
5. In *Paul Eluard* (Poètes d'aujourd'hui, 1), ed. by Louis Parrot (Paris, 1958).
6. *Ibid.*, p. 135.

7. *Ibid.*, p. 207.

8. Pierre Emmanuel, *Le je universel chez Paul Eluard* (Paris, 1948), especially p. 17.

9. Charles Baudelaire, *OEuvres complètes* (Paris, 1951), p. 1076.

Chapter Three

1. In *Paul Eluard* (Poètes d'aujourd'hui, 1), ed. by Louis Parrot (Paris, 1958).

2. On the significance of light in Eluard's poetry, see Robert Nugent, "Eluard's Use of Light," *French Review*, XXXIV (May, 1961), 525–30.

3. In *Paul Eluard* (Poètes d'aujourd'hui, 1).

4. *Ibid.*

5. *Ibid.*

6. *Ibid.*

7. Charles Baudelaire, "Fusées," in *OEuvres complètes* (Paris, 1951), p. 1189.

8. *Ibid.*

9. For a discussion of "Première du monde," cf. Wallace Fowlie, "Eluard: the doctrine of love," in *The Age of Surrealism* (Denver and New York, 1950), especially pp. 147–50.

10. Victor Hugo, *William Shakespeare* (Paris, 1864), p. 140.

11. In *Paul Eluard* (Poètes d'aujourd'hui, 1).

12. *Ibid.*

13. *Ibid.*

14. Paul Eluard, *Les Sentiers et les routes de la poèsie* (Paris, [1952] 1954), p. 173.

Chapter Four

1. Paul Valéry, *OEuvres*, I (Paris, 1957), 1321.

2. Jules Supervielle, "En songeant à un art poétique," *Naissances* (Paris, 1934), pp. 57–58.

3. Balakian, *op. cit.*, p. 104. I have followed her discussion of Hegel's influence on Surrealism (Balakian, *op. cit.*, pp. 103–10).

4. The following quotation from Stace is helpful in understanding Hegel's notion of the Absolute: "The first mode in which the mind apprehends the Absolute is, in accordance with general principles, in *immediacy*. Since the content of all modes of apprehending the Absolute is the same, viz., the Absolute itself, this immediacy must attach to the *form* under which it is apprehended. At first, therefore, the Absolute will be manifested under the guise of immediacy, that

is to say, under the guise of external sense-objects. The shining of the Absolute, or the Idea, though the veils of the sense-world—this is beauty. It is essential to the idea of beauty that its object be sensuous—an actual thing present to the senses, as a staue, a building, or the beautiful sound of music, or at least it should be the mental image of a sensuous object, as in poetry. It must be individual and concrete. It cannot be an abstraction. The beautiful object thus addresses itself to the senses. But it also addresses itself to the mind or spirit. For a mere sensuous existence, as such, is not beautiful. Only when the mind perceives the Idea shining through it is it beautiful." W. T. Stace, *The Philosophy of Hegel: A Systematic Exposition* (London. 1924), p. 443.

5. Balakian, *op. cit.*, p. 125.

6. Quoted in Marcel Jean, *The History of Surrealist Painting* (New York, 1960), p. 207.

7. *Ibid.*

8. In *Paul Eluard* (Poètes d'aujourd'hui, 1).

9. Michel Carrouges, *Eluard et Claudel* (Paris, 1945), p. 41.

10. Paul Eluard, *Capitale de la douleur* (Paris, 1926), p. 41.

11. Perche, *op. cit.*, p. 47.

Chapter Five

1. Charles Baudelaire, *OEuvres complètes* (Paris, 1951), p. 1092.

2. *Ibid.*, p. 1189.

3. Jules Laforgue, "Lettre à C. Henry, décembre, 1881," *OEuvres complètes*, IV (Paris, 1925), 66.

4. ————, "Lettre à Madame Mullezer, 18 juillet, 1882," *OEuvres complètes*, IV (Paris, 1925), 182.

5. Cf. the following statement by Fontenelle: *Quoi! ce qu'il y a de plus estimable en nous*, sera-ce donc ce qui dépendra le moins de nous, *ce qui agira le plus en nous sans nous-mêmes, ce qui aura le plus de conformité avec l'instinct des animaux? Car cet enthousiasme et cette fureur bien expliqués se réduisent à de véritables instincts.* Quoted in Henri Bremond, *Prière et poésie* (Paris, 1926), p. 26.

6. Charles Baudelaire, *op. cit.*, p. 1078.

7. *Ibid.*, pp. 287–88.

8. Cf. the following statement by André Breton in *Du Surréalisme en ses oeuvres vives* (1953): *L'attitude du surréalisme à l'égard de la nature est commandée avant tout par la conception initiale qu'il s'est faite de l'image poétique.* Quoted by Robert Gibson, *ed., Modern French Poets on Poetry* (Cambridge, 1961), p. 178.

9. Paul Eluard, *Les Sentiers et les routes de la poésie* (Paris, 1954), p. 16.

10. Cf. the following statement by Breton, *op. cit.*: *On sait qu'il y a vu le moyen d'obtenir, dans des conditions d'extrême détente bien mieux que d'extrême concentration de l'esprit, certains traits de feu reliant deux éléments de la réalité de catégories si éloignées l'une de l'autre que la raison se refuserait à les mettre en rapport et qu'il faut s'être défait momentanément de tout esprit critique pour leur permettre de se confronter.* Quoted in Gibson, *op. cit.*

11. Cf. the following statement by Breton, *op. cit*: *Cet extraordinaire gréement d'étincelles, dès l'instant où l'on a surpris le mode de génération et où l'on a pris conscience de ses inépuisables ressources, mène l'esprit à se faire du monde et de lui-même une représentation moins opaque.* Quoted in Gibson, *op. cit.*, pp. 178–79.

12. Quoted by Perche, *op. cit.*, p. 84.

13. Cf. the following statement by Breton, *op. cit.*: *Il [le poète] vérifie, alors, fragmentairement il est vrai, du moins par lui-même, que "tout ce qui est en haut est comme ce qui est en bas" et tout ce qui est dedans comme tout ce qui est en dehors. Le monde, à partir de là, s'offre à lui comme un cryptogramme qui ne demeure indéchiffrable qu'autant que l'on n'est pas rompu à la gymnastique acrobatique permettant à volonté de dépasser d'un après à l'autre.* Quoted in Gibson, *op. cit.*, p. 179.

14. Cf. the following statement by Breton, *op. cit.*: *On n'insistera jamais trop sur le fait que la métaphore, bénéficiant de toute licence dans le surréalisme, laisse loin derrière elle l'analogie (préfabriquée). . . . Bien que toutes deux tombent d'accord pour honorer le système des "correspondances," il y a de l'une à l'autre la distance qui sépare le haut vol du terre-à-terre.* Quoted in Gibson, *op. cit.*

15. Cf. Staffen Bergsten, *Time and Eternity: A Study in the Structure and Symbolism of T. S. Eliot's Four Quartets* (Stockholm, 1960), p. 137.

16. Michel Carrouges, *op. cit.*, p. 44.

17. Paul Eluard, *Capitale de la douleur* (Paris, 1926), p. 12.

Chapter Six

1. For a discussion on *Unanimisme*, see the article in the *Dictionary of French Literature*, ed. by Sidney D. Braun (New York, 1958).

2. "Poésie ininterrompue" is also found in *The Selected Writings of Paul Eluard*, with English translations by Lloyd Alexander and introductory notes by Aragon, Louis Parrot and Claude Roy (Norfolk, Conn., *n. d.*).

3. Aragon, "Uninterrupted Poetry," in *The Selected Writings of Paul Eluard*, tr. by Lloyd Alexander, p. xi.

4. *Ibid.*, p. xii.

5. Pierre Emmanuel, *op. cit.*, p. 11.

6. *Ibid.*

7. *Ibid.* p. 17.

8. Paul Claudel, "Réflexions et propositions sur le vers français," *Réflexions sur la poésie* (Paris, 1963), p. 33.

9. T. S. Eliot, "The Social Function of Poetry (1945)," in *Critiques and Essays in Criticism*, 1920–1948, selected by R. W. Stallman (New York, 1949), p. 107.

Chapter Seven

1. Arthur Rimbaud, "Lettre du 15 mai 1871," *OEuvres complètes* (Paris, 1946), pp. 254–55.

2. Cf. Edward Zeller, *Outlines of the History of Greek Philosophy* (New York, 1955), p. 64: "For he [Heraclitus] was the first philosopher to recognize the symbolic character of religion . . . the way to which seemed in some instances to be pointed out by language."

3. For the discussion that follows, see Michael Hamburger, *Reason and Energy: Studies in German Literature* (New York, 1957), p. 100.

4. Pierre Emmanuel, *op. cit.*, p. 24.

5. *Ibid.*

6. Walt Whitman, *Poems and Prose*, selected with notes by Mark Van Doren (New York, 1945), p. 16.

7. *Ibid.*, p. 17.

8. Victor Hugo, *op. cit.*, p. 142.

9. ――――, "Préface" to the *Odes et Ballades*, 1822.

Chapter Eight

1. Percy Bysshe Shelley, "A Defence of Poetry," *The Prose Works. . . .* Vol. II (New York, 1925), 32.

Selected Bibliography

PRIMARY SOURCES

The standard text is that of the Pléiade edition: Paul Eluard, *OEuvres complètes*, Préface et chronologie de Lucien Scheler, textes établis et annotés par Marcelle Dumas et Lucien Scheler. Paris: Gallimard, 2 vols., 1968. A selection of poems is that of the series *Poètes d'aujourd'hui* (no. 1): Paul Eluard, *Choix de poèmes, portraits, facsimilé, documents, inédits*. Nouvelle éd. augmentée, préface de Louis Parrot, postface de Jean Marcenac. Paris: Seghers, 1958. Another selection of poems is that published by Gallimard (Paris, 1951). Primary biographical source material is found in *Paul Eluard par lui-même*, ed. Raymond Jean (Ecrivains de toujours, no. 79): Paris: Ed. du Seuil, 1968; *Eluard, livre d'identité*, ed. Robert D. Valette:: Paris: Tchou, 1967.

Mourir de ne pas mourir. Paris: Gallimard, 1924.
Capitale de la douleur. Paris: Gallimard, 1926.
L'Amour la poésie. Paris: Gallimard, 1929.
L'Immaculée conception. Paris: Editions surréalistes de José Corti, 1930. (With André Breton). Réédition, Seghers, 1961.
La Vie immédiate. Paris: Editions des Cahiers libres, 1932.
La Rose publique. Paris: Gallimard, 1934.
Facile. Paris: G.L.M., 1936.
Notes sur la poésie: Paris: G.L.M., 1935.
Les Yeux fertiles. Paris: G.L.M., 1936.
Cours naturel. Paris: Editions du Sagittaire, 1938.
Chanson complète. Paris: Gallimard, 1939.
Donner à voir. Paris: Gallimard, 1939.
Le Livre ouvert, I, 1938–1940. Paris: Editions des Cahiers d'art, 1940.
Le Livre ouvert, II, 1939–1941. Paris: Editions des Cahiers d'art, 1942.
Au rendez-vous allemand. Paris: Editions de minuit, 1944.
Poésie ininterrompue. Paris: Gallimard, 1946.
Le Dur Désir de durer. Paris: Editions Arnold-Borda, 1946.
Corps mémorable. Paris: Seghers, 1948.
Poèmes politiques. Paris: Gallimard, 1948.

Les Sentiers et les routes de la poésie. Lyon: Les écrivains réunis Armand Henneuse, 1952. (Réédition, Gallimard, 1954).

SECONDARY SOURCES

ALEXANDER, LLOYD, trans. *Paul Eluard: Selected writings.* With English translations . . . and introductory notes by Aragon, Louis Parrot and Claude Roy (Norfolk, Conn.: A New Directions Book, *n. d.*). Poems arranged chronologically, most of them late poems (after 1938). French text with translation *en face.* Study by Aragon stresses the humanitarian and social interest of Eluard.

BALAKIAN, ANNA. "Post-Surrealism of Aragon and Eluard," in *Surrealism and the Road to the Absolute* (New York: The Noonday Press, 1959), pp. 165–87. Very important essay. Aragon and Eluard gave up the search for the absolute ("metaphysical vision") in favor of a partisan poetry. This compromise brought about the disappearance of the Surrealist linguistic achievement.

BOGAN, LOUISE. "The Poetry of Paul Eluard," in *Selected Criticism: Prose and Poetry* (New York: The Noonday Press, 1955), pp. 157–70. Eluard's most distinctive quality is his pathos (*pathéthique*), forced by the tough spirit of the time to act as the "unconscious" and to function under manifestos.

CARMODY, FRANCIS J. "Eluard's Rupture with Surrealism," *PMLA,* LXXXVI, 4 (Sept., 1961), 436–46. Analyzes the factors contributing to Eluard's rupture with Breton in 1938 other than a change from Surrealism to Stalinism: Eluard's *fatigue* with Breton's pacifism and with his manner of dream interpretation. This rupture forecast by the change in poetic themes and techniques, later brought to fruition in *Poésie ininterrompue* (1945).

CARROUGES, MICHEL. *Eluard et Claudel* (Paris: Editions du Seuil, 1945). Contains "La Symbolique d'Eluard," underlying the dual aspect of Eluard's achievement: joyful acceptance of life and revolt against the universe, earthiness and intellectuality, enthusiasm and despair, all accompanied by a feeling of love which gives the poetry an incomparable charm.

CAWS, MARY ANN. "Paul Eluard," in *The Poetry of Dada and Surrealism* (Princeton: Princeton Univ. Press, 1970), pp. 136–69. Finds the themes of purity, spontaneity, and intensity equally important as in Tzara and Breton. Stresses the Surrealist dualism in Eluard, the opaque and the transparent, the dark and the visionary light.

EGLIN, HEINRICH. *Liebe und Inspiration im Werke von Paul Eluard* (Bern: Francke Verlag, 1965). The three experiences of love in

Eluard's poetry: Gala (the impossibility of direct love); the "Queen of Diamonds" (the dream love); Nusch ("the possibility of showing what man loves").

EMMANUEL, PIERRE. *Le je universel chez Eluard* (Paris: GLM, 1948). An *examen symbolique* of Eluard's verse, which derives from the "infinite metamorphoses of appearances"; underscores the Protean quality of Eluard's imagery.

FOWLIE, WALLACE. "Eluard: the Doctrine of Love," in *Age of Surrealism* (Denver and New York: The Swallow Press and William Morrow, 1940), pp. 138–56. Defines the Surrealist view on love as a part of the search for poetic purity, liberty in human activities, the revelation of the inner spirit of man in the Surrealist techniques of free association.

————. "Paul Eluard," in *Mid-Century French Poets* (New York: Grove Press, 1955), pp. 170–97. The introduction to the translation of selected poems defines the "miracle" of Eluard's poetry in terms of the extremes it contains, especially intimacy contrasted with a collective consciousness of man in present society.

GAFFÉ, RENÉ. *Paul Eluard* (Paris et Bruxelle: A l'enseigne du cheval ailé, 1945). Each work discussed in the order of publication. Discusses Eluard's importance for poetic languages; stresses Eluard as a poet of the Resistance.

INGRASSI, ANTONIN. *Eluard et Baudelaire* (Aix-en-Provence: La Pensée universitaire, 1962). Traces influences of Baudelaire's literary doctrines on Eluard.

JEAN, MARCEL. *The History of Surrealist Painting*, trans. by Simon Watson Tyler (New York: Grove Press, 1960). Important references to Eluard's participation in the Surrealist movement in painting; especially useful for understanding the aesthetic principles common to both Surrealist painting and Surrealist literature.

KITTANG, ATLE. *D'Amour la poésie: l'univers des métamorphoses dans l'oeuvre surréaliste de Paul Eluard*, (Situations, no. 12), Paris: Lettres modernes Minard, 1969. Traces Eluard's poetry until 1938; early poetry an *attente de l'Inconnu*. After 1938, poetry become circumstantial though still personal in terms of Eluard's failure to find the Unknown.

LIPPARD, LUCY R., ed. *Surrealists on Art* (Englewood Cliffs, N.J.: Prentice-Hall, 1970). Introductory essay on Surrealist aesthetic, contains translation from *Donner à voir*.

MATTHEWS, J. H. *An Introduction to Surrealism* (University Park, Pa.: Pennsylvania State Univ. Press, 1965). A major history of the Surrealist movement, the continuing presence of its aesthetic, Eluard's contributions to Surrealism.

MEURAUD, MARYVONNE. *L'Image végétale dans la poésie d'Eluard*, (Langues et styles, no. 4). Paris: Lettres modernes Minard, 1966. Process of humanization in Eluard's poetry achieved through an awareness and understanding of links between nature and human beings (the poet, the woman he loves).

NADEAU, MAURICE. *Histoire du surréalisme, suivie de documents surréalistes* (Paris: Editions du Seuil, 1964). The first part gives the history of the Surrealist movement; the second part, the documents of Surrealism, followed by a bibliography. Indispensable for study of movement and Eluard's contribution to the Surrealist revolution.

NUGENT, ROBERT. "Eluard's Use of Light," *French Review*, XXXIV, 6 (May, 1961). Eluard's use of images of light as points around which he centers his convictions (love, political and humanitarian concerns, poetry).

PARROT, LOUIS, ed. *Paul Eluard: Choix de poèmes . . .* (Paris: Seghers, 1952). Study of the evolution of Eluard's poetry with biographical references, first published in 1948. Later edition emphasizes the humanitarian, post-Resistance character of Eluard's work.

PERCHE, LOUIS. *Paul Eluard*, (Classiques du XXe siècle). Paris: Editions universitaires, 1963. A thematic study of Eluard's work (images, reality, sensations, ethical values). Contains a useful bibliography of Eluard's work and references to it.

PEYRE, HENRI. "Paul Eluard: 'A peine défigurée,' 'Amoureuse,' 'Le baiser,' 'Couvre-feu,' 'La dame de carreau,' 'Je cache les sombres trésors,' " in BRADSHAW, STANLEY, ed. *The Poem in Itself* (New York: Holt, Rinehart and Winston, 1960), pp. 104–9. Detailed close reading of the poems (images, poetic intent, vocabulary).

RAYMOND, MARCEL. *De Baudelaire au surréalisme* (Paris: José Corti, 1947). Especially valuable is Chap. VI, "Les Poètes surréalistes." Discusses poetic purity, the notion of the absolute, poetic inspiration in Eluard as they emerge from the current of aesthetic concepts from Baudelaire on.

SHOWALTER, ENGLISH, JR. "Biographical Aspects of Eluard's Poetry," *PMLA*, LXXVIII, 3 (June, 1963), 280–86. Eluard's poems are not "isolated and impersonal anthology pieces," but a record of Eluard's spiritual life and triumph over despair. Stresses the need for a knowledge of biography to understand the poetry.

Index

(The works of Eluard are listed under his name.)

151